Also from The New Press and SIUniverse Me

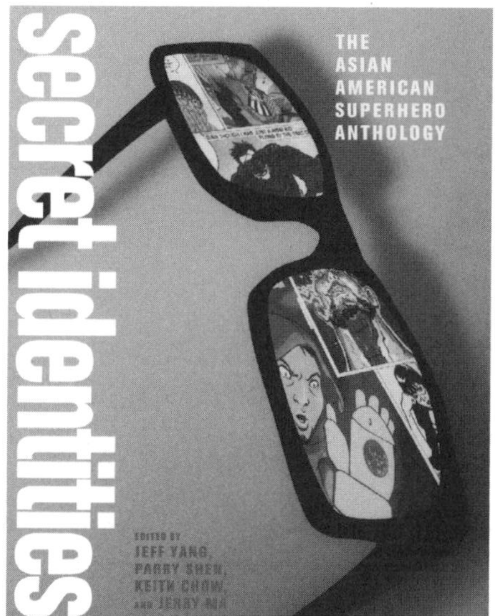

Secret Identities: The Asian American Superhero Anthology

Vowee!!! What mind-blowing superheroes exploding out of the pages of *Secret Identities*! s a kid who grew up on comics in the '40s and '50s, for the first time in my life, I recognized, entified, and became a comic book hero."

—George Takei, actor

s a comics fan, I had a great time reading all the fabulous tales; as an Asian American comics professional, am more than a little in awe of the amazing talent assembled under one house."

—Jim Lee, artist and co-publisher of DC Comics

hese Asian American superheroes knocked me out! I wish I had known these superheroes when I was kid—I'd have traded my entire comic book collection for this butt-kicking, death-defying, and brilliant nthology."

—Helen Zia, author of *Asian American Dreams: The Emergence of an American People*

ecret Identities has hit upon one of those truths that feels surprising only because no one thought of it oner: that our culture's superhero template dovetails uncannily with Asian American issues and identity."

—David Henry Hwang, playwright (*M. Butterfly, Golden Child*)

Published in the United States by The New Press, New York, 2012
Distributed by Perseus Distribution

CIP data available.

ISBN 978-1-59558-824-1 (pbk.)

Now in its twentieth year, The New Press publishes books that promote and enrich public discussion and understanding of th issues vital to our democracy and to a more equitable world. These books are made possible by the enthusiasm of our reader the support of a committed group of donors, large and small; the collaboration of our many partners in the independent me and the not-for-profit sector; booksellers, who often hand-sell New Press books; librarians; and above all by our authors.

www.thenewpress.com

Book design and composition by Jerry Ma and Tak Toyoshima

Printed in the United States of America

10 9 8 7 6 5 4 3 2 1

SHATTERED

THE ASIAN AMERICAN COMICS ANTHOLOGY · A SECRET IDENTITIES BOOK

EDITOR IN CHIEF: JEFF YANG • MANAGING EDITOR: PARRY SHEN
EDITOR AT LARGE: KEITH CHOW • ART DIRECTOR: JERRY MA
SENIOR GRAPHIC DESIGNER: TAK TOYOSHIMA • SENIOR ARTIST: GLENN URIETA

www.secretidentities.org • @siuniverse • www.thenewpress.com

CONTENTS

PROLOGUE

1 **THE SACRIFICE*** — Story: JEFF YANG, PARRY SHEN & KEITH CHOW • Art: JERRY MA
3 BURN — Story: JIMMY MA • Art: JERRY MA

CHAPTER ONE: THE BRUTE

13 **DRIVING STEEL: THE BREAKING** — Story: JEFF YANG • Art: KRISHNA M. SADASIVAM
23 MASTER TORTOISE & MASTER HARE — Story: HOWARD WONG • Art: JAMIE NOGUCHI
27 SHOWTIME — Story & Art: BERNARD CHANG
31 SOLITARY — Story: MICHAEL KANG & EDMUND LEE • Art: GLENN URIETA
41 CLEAN GETAWAY — Story: JAMIE FORD • Art: A.L. BAROZA

CHAPTER TWO: THE TEMPTRESS

43 **BAI BAI, BAI TSAI** — Story: JEFF YANG • Art: MARTIN HSU & SOPHIA LIN
53 CHING SHIH: QUEEN OF PIRATES* — Story: NATALIE KIM • Art: ROBIN HA
59 THE REGRETS WE TALK ABOUT — Story & Art: FRED CHAO
64 HEROES WITHOUT A COUNTRY: TOKYO ROSE* — Story: DANIEL JAI LEE • Art: DAFU YU
72 THE DATE* — Story: AMY CHU • Art: LARRY HAMA & CRAIG YEUNG

GALLERY

75 ADAM WARROCK — Story: EUGENE AHN • Art: MING DOYLE
76 REVOLUTION SHUFFLE — Story: BAO PHI • Art: GB TRAN
77 TEMPEST — Story: KAI MA • Art: ERIC KIM
78 THE WALKMAN — Story: AARON TAKAHASHI • Art: MUKESH SINGH
79 ANGRY ASIAN MAN — Story: PHIL YU • Art: JERRY MA
80 MEI THE ALIEN — Story: KOJI STEVEN SAKAI • Art: DEODATO PANGANDOYON
81 CAMP MECH — Story: ERIC NAKAMURA • Art: SARA SAEDI
82 THE DEATH STALKER — Story: THENMOZHI SOUNDARARAJAN • Art: SAUMIN SURESH PATEL

CHAPTER THREE: THE BRAIN

83 **HIDE AND SIKH** — Story: PARRY SHEN • Art: JEREMY ARAMBULO
93 THE POWER OF PETUNIA — Story: JOY OSMANSKI • Art: YASMIN LIANG
97 DRONES AND DROIDS — Story: PAUL WEI • Art: CHI-YUN LAU
99 CAMDEN'S REVENGE — Story: KEIKO AGENA • Art: LOUIE CHIN
105 METATRON — Story & Art: STUART NG
109 LOS ROBOS, ARIZONA** — Story: GREG PAK • Art: TAKESHI MIYAZAWA
119 A CUT ABOVE — Story: JAMIE FORD • Art: A.L. BAROZA

CHAPTER FOUR: THE ALIEN

121 **PERIL: WELCOME TO THE TERROR** — Story: KEITH CHOW • Art: JEF CASTRO
131 MISS MOTI, SHATTERED — Story & Art: KRIPA JOSHI
132 THE STRANGER — Story & Art: JOHANN CHOI
135 PERSONAL MONSTERS — Story & Art: TRACI HONDA
139 WEIGHTLESS — Story: TANUJ CHOPRA • Art: ALICE MEICHI LI
143 A DREAM OF FLYING* — Story: A. VERONICA WONG & R. SUAREZ • Art: CHRISTINE NORRIE & CRAIG YEUNG
151 FASHION NEVER DYES — Story: JAMIE FORD • Art: A.L. BAROZA

CHAPTER FIVE: THE MANIPULATOR

153 **HIBAKUSHA: SECRETS*** — Story: PARRY SHEN • Art: SEAN CHEN
165 PUSH* — Story: JENNIFER S. FANG • Art: ACE CONTINUADO & JULIAN SAN JUAN
173 PERSONS OF MASS DESTRUCTION* — Story: GARY JACKSON • Art: CESAR P. CASTILLO JR
179 THE MERCIFUL* — Story: REN HSIEH • Art: BRYAN LEE
183 QI LAI!* — Story: ROGER MA • Art: DHEERAJ VERMA & TAK TOYOSHIMA
193 OCCUPY ETHNIC FOODS — Story & Art: TAK TOYOSHIMA
195 SHADOW HERO — Story: GENE LUEN YANG • Art: SONNY LIEW

FINALE

198 **THE SEALING*** — Story: JEFF YANG, PARRY SHEN & KEITH CHOW • Art: GLENN URIETA

EPILOGUE

209 **THE VILCEK STORY** — Story: JEFF YANG • Art: WENDY XU

COVER ILLUSTRATION BY: CLIFF CHIANG

* LETTERED BY JANICE CHIANG
** LETTERED BY SIMON BOWLAND

CONTRIBUTORS

iko Agena
‹eikoAgena • keikoagena.com

gene Ahn
ugewarrock • adamwarrock.com

remy Arambulo
eremyArambulo • jeremyarambulo.com

.. Baroza
.LBaroza • rose-madder.com

non Bowland
iimonBowland

sar P. Castillo Jr.
enbuildplay.com

f Castro
cretidentities.org/Site/Jef_Castro

rnard Chang
nebernardchang • bernardchang.com

d Chao
dchao.com

an Chen
anchen.com

ff Chiang
liffchiang • cliffchiang.com

nice Chiang
ebook.com/JaniceChiangComicLetterer

uie Chin
oubot • louiechin.com

hann Choi
cretidentities.org

uj Chopra
ChopsFilms • chopsfilms.com

ith Chow
ne_real_chow • lokblogging.blogspot.com

y Chu
myChu • nerdygal.com

e Continuado
e-continuado.daportfolio.com

ng Doyle
ningdoyle • mingdoyle.com

nifer S. Fang
eappropriate • reappropriate.co

nie Ford
amieFord • jamieford.com

bin Ha
in.megaten.net

ry Hama
vurl.com/LarryHamaFB

ci Honda
cihonda.com

n Hsieh
heRealRenHsieh • dynastyproject.org

Martin Hsu
@martinhsu • martinhsu.com

Gary Jackson
facebook.com/garyallenjackson

Kripa Joshi
@kripakreations • kripakreations.com

Michael Kang
@kangisman • kangisman.com

Eric Kim
@inkskratch • inkskratch.com

Natalie Kim
@NatalieKimNYC • nataliekim.com

Chi-Yun Lau
@DrCl4w • chi-yun.com

Bryan Lee
bchongle.daportfolio.com

Daniel Jai Lee
@danieljailee

Edmund Lee
@edmundlee

Alice Meichi Li
@AliceMeichi • alicemeichi.com

Yasmin Liang
@yasminliang • yazmeanie.com

Sonny Liew
@sonnyliew • sonnyliew.com

Sophia Lin
sophialin.net

Jerry Ma
@epicprops • epicprops.com

Jimmy Ma
epicprops.com

Kai Ma
@kai_ma • opencitymag.com

Roger Ma
@zombiecombat • zombiecombatclub.com

Takeshi Miyazawa
@takmiyazawa • takeshimiyazawa.com

Eric Nakamura
@giantroboteric • giantrobot.com

Stuart Ng
@kurenex • genesoul.com

Jamie Noguchi
@angryzenmaster • ypcomic.com

Christine Norrie
@christinenorrie • christinenorrie.com

Joy Osmanski
@joyosmanski • joyosmanski.com

Greg Pak
@gregpak • gregpak.com

Deodato Pangandoyon
deodatoart.blogspot.com

Saumin Suresh Patel
pictorialcinema.blogspot.com

Bao Phi
baophi.com

Krishna M. Sadasivam
@pcweenies • pcweenies.com

Sara Saedi
sarasaedi.com

Koji Steven Sakai
@ksakai1

Julian San Juan
facebook.com/HULIYAN

Parry Shen
@parryshen • parryshen.com

Mukesh Singh
@ubermensch76 • nisachar.deviantart.com

Thenmozhi Soundararajan
@dalitdiva

Reinhardt Suarez
theporkchopexpress.com

Aaron Takahashi
imdb.com/name/nm0847099/

Tak Toyoshima
@TakToyoshima • secretasianman.com

GB Tran
@vietnamerica • gbtran.com

Glenn Urieta
glennurieta.com

Dheeraj Verma
dheerajverma.com

Paul Wei
maxwellwong.com

Howard Wong
@howardwong1 • howard-wong.blogspot.com

Angela Veronica Wong
@veratristan • angelaveronicawong.com

Wendy Xu
@littlewendycat • angrygirlcomics.tumblr.com

Gene Luen Yang
@geneluenyang • geneluenyang.com

Jeff Yang
@originalspin • originalspin.posterous.com

Craig Yeung
@csyeung • csyeung1.blogspot.com

DaFu Yu
@DaFuMonkeyquest • dafuyu.deviantart.com

Phil Yu
@angryasianman • angryasianman.com

ACKNOWLEDGMENTS

The editors would like to give special thanks to Tak Toyoshima, Glenn Urieta, and Janice Chiang, whose talent and hard work, above and beyond the call of duty, were critical to making this book happen; Joyce Li, Rick Kinsel, and Jan and Marica Vilcek of the Vilcek Foundation, for believing i and funding this project; Sarah Fan, our editor, for her unflagging support and patience; and our families, without whom we're nothing.

HOW TO READ THIS BOOK

Each chapter of *Shattered* collects together unrelated stories that seek to reimagine one of five archetypes frequently associated with Asians in media and popular culture: The Brute, the Brain, the Temptress, the Alien, and the Manipulator. The chapters are introduced by sections of a singl long tale that tells of mankind's secret fight with the fiendish beings behind those archetypes. To follow that narrative, read those sections back to back, in order, beginning with the Prologue and ending with the Finale.

For updates on the Secret Identities Universe, to download discussion guides about issues and themes raised in this book, or to bring the SI Universe Tour to your school or organization, visit www.secretidentities.org. Follow us on Twitter at @siuniverse.

BENEATH WU TANG MOUNTAIN, CHINA. 1733 A.D.
YOU HAVE DONE WELL, DISCIPLES. YOU ARE STRONG IN MIND, BODY, AND WILL; FEW HUMAN OPPONENTS COULD STAND AGAINST YOU. BUT IT IS TIME I SHARED WITH YOU OUR ORDER'S GREATEST SECRET.
LOOK DEEP INTO THE MIRROR OF DIVINE IMMORTALS; THE GLASS UPON WHICH YOU HAVE CONTEMPLATED SO MANY HOURS DURING OUR TIME TOGETHER.
THIS TIME, HOWEVER, IT WILL NOT REFLECT YOURSELVES—BUT THE FACES OF YOUR TRUE ENEMIES...
BROTHERS!
YOU DARE CALL US THAT, DARK ONE?
YOU WHO TORMENT US?
YOU WHO MAKE US DANCE UPON YOUR STRINGS?
I AM "BROTHER" TO NO ONE—LEAST OF ALL TO YOU, SHADOWLURKER.
BO-KWUN, THE MANIPULATOR
KUM-SAU, THE BRUTE
ZHI-LIK, THE BRAIN
YI-HEUNG, THE ALIEN
NGAU-YUN, THE TEMPTRESS
TOGETHER WE AWOKE. TOGETHER WE EMERGED FROM THE BLACK WOMB OF CHAOS. TOGETHER WE SLEW AND CONSUMED OUR LESSER KIN. WE FIVE ARE JOINED BY BLOOD AND FURY, BY FIRE AND FEAR, AND BY THE HUNGER THAT STILL TEARS AT OUR HEARTS.
AND SO I CALL YOU SIBLINGS, AND, IN DOING SO, BID YOU LISTEN TO WHAT I HAVE TO SHARE.
"A GREAT WALL BARS US FROM THE MORTAL WORLD, THROUGH WHICH LEAKS THE MEREST TASTE OF HUMANITY."
"ZHI-LIK, YOU HAVE GRAZED ON THEIR SCHEMING ENVY."
"YI-HEUNG, YOU HAVE GORGED ON THEIR NAMELESS DREAD."
"KUM-SAU, YOU HAVE FED UPON THEIR SEETHING RAGE."
"AND NGAU-YUN, YOU HAVE BATTENED ON THEIR FURTIVE LUST."
"BUT WHAT WE CONSUME IS MERELY AN APPETIZER. THE FULL FEAST LIES IN THE WORLD BEYOND."
"SO I ASK YOU TO JOIN ME, MY SIBLINGS. FOR I HAVE FOUND A WEAKNESS IN THE WALL THAT OUR COMBINED POWER CAN PIERCE."
"JOIN ME...FOR A BANQUET OF SOULS AWAITS."

THERE IS FEAR IN YOUR EYES? THERE SHOULD BE. THE NG DUK, THE FIVE VENOMS, ARE FEARFUL CREATURES.
BUT... THEIR ASSAULT ON OUR WORLD WAS STOPPED, AND THEIR POWER SEALED. FOR NOW.
"IT TOOK THE COMBINED POWERS OF TWO OF THIS WORLD'S GREATEST HEROES TO DO SO: MY MASTER, ZHANG SANFENG, AND SAO TUALUN – A MEMBER OF ONE OF EARTH'S ELDER RACES, THE ELEMENTAL BEINGS WE CALL THE DJINN."
"FOR SEVEN DAYS AND NIGHTS, MASTER ZHANG AND MASTER SAO FOUGHT THE NG DUK, SEEKING TO PUSH THEM BACK BEFORE THEY FULLY MANIFESTED IN THIS REALM."
"THEY SUCCEEDED. BUT TO ACHIEVE TRUE VICTORY, THEY HAD TO CLOSE THE GATE THE DEMONS HAD MADE."
"AND FOR T THEY PA A TERRIB COST.
"THE MASTERS GAVE THEIR LIVES TO BAR THE NG DUK FROM OUR WORLD."
"BUT THE POWER OF THE SEAL CAN ONLY BE MAINTAINED IF FUELED BY THE FORCE OF WILL."
AND NOW, MY STUDENTS, I AM OLD. I WILL NOT BE LONG IN THIS WORLD.
THERE MUST BE ONE AMONG YOU WHO WILL TAKE THE KEEPING OF THE MIRROR UPON HIMSELF.
LET THIS BURDEN BE MINE, MASTER.
LIN. THE YOUNGEST OF OUR ORDER, THE LEAST TRAINED, THE LEAST DISCIPLINED. YET... I BELIEVE YOU ARE THE PROPER CHOICE.
"THE NG DUK WILL TEMPT YOU. THEY WILL ATTEMPT TO BLIND YOUR EYES, TO CRACK YOUR WILL, TO TWIST YOUR SOUL."
"BUT YOU MUST STAND FIRM, L
"BECAUSE IF YOU FALTER. ALL IS LOS
NEXT CHAPTER: "THE BRUTE"
DRIVING STEEL: THE BREAKING

BURN

STORY: JIMMY MA
ART: JERRY MA

"TELL HIM THE *CHAMPION* OF THE *WEST* IS *HERE* FOR HIS COUNTRY."

MY FATHER WAS A SCHOLAR AND A WARRIOR.

THEY CALLED HIM THE *COMMISSIONER*.
SOME CALLED HIM THE GREATEST MAN IN CHINA.

"COURAGE AND COMPASSION IN EQUAL PARTS," HE ALWAYS TOLD ME.
BUT THIS WAS THE FIRST TIME...

"I SAW *FEAR* ON HIS FACE."

HE TOLD ME OF HIS PAST WITH THE *FLOWER*.
HOW HE HAD TOUCHED DARKNESS AND BECOME *NOTHING*.
LESS THAN A COWARD.
SOON, MORE AND MORE OF OUR PEOPLE STARTED BREATHING WITH THE FLOWER.

THE COMMISSIONER FOLLOWED THE PATH OF DISCIPLINE TO FREE HIMSELF.
HARMONY OF MIND AND BODY.
THE PATH BEATEN BY GENERATIONS OF OUR ANCESTORS.
THEN HE FOUND HE HAD UNLOCKED A *SPECIAL* ABILITY.
HE HAD TAPPED A RESERVOIR OF *STRENGTH* FUELED BY THE *UNITY* OF THE PEOPLE.

WHEN YOUR FATHER FIGHTS FOR THE PEOPLE, HIS STRENGTH *INCREASES* AS THEIR BELIEF IN HIM GROWS.

BUT THE STRANGER HAS FOOLED MANY INTO BELIEVING THAT *YOU* ARE AN *ENEMY* OF THE STATE.

WILL YOU BE WEAKER IF YOU FIGHT HIM NOW?
I HAVE *ALWAYS* BEEN FIGHTING TO UNIFY THE PEOPLE, SON.
WEAK OR NOT, I *MUST* CONFRONT THIS ENEMY.

HE IS ELUSIVE AND POWERFUL AND HE'S BEEN A PART OF ME FOR TOO LONG.
EVEN IF I FIGHT ALONE TODAY, I *MUST* DEFEAT THIS DEMON.

I KNEW YOU WOULD COME WHEN I CALLED, COMMISSIONER.
YOU'RE FAR TOO OBLIGING TO TURN DOWN AN INVITATION FROM THE *CHAMPION* OF THE WEST.
BUT IS IT *REALLY* ME YOU'RE RESPONDING TO?
I THINK IT'S SOMETHING *ELSE*.
YOU WANT TO WRITE YOUR HISTORY TODAY.
CHANGE YOUR FATE.

THE STRANGER SPOKE OF HISTORY THAT DAY...
AS IF IT HAD ALREADY BEEN WRITTEN.
WE'D ALREADY DUG OUR OWN *GRAVES*.
AND THE LIES HAD ALREADY BEEN TOLD.
THE BATTLE WAS EVENLY FOUGHT...
BUT FOR *ONE* ADVANTAGE.

POISON.
ONCE YOU LET IT IN...
...IT BECOMES A PART OF YOU.
PERHAPS MY FATHER WAS BESTED NOT ONLY BY THE STRANGER...
...BUT BY HIMSELF AS WELL.

HERE WERE *CONFLICTING* REPORTS OF THE EVENTS OF THAT DAY.

SOME SAID THE COMMISSIONER WAS NO MATCH FOR THE CHAMPION OF THE WEST.

逆

OTHERS, THAT HE WAS DEVOURED BY A *DEMON*.

NO ONE COULD *TRULY* BELIEVE HE WAS A TRAITOR.

NO ONE KNEW WHAT TO BELIEVE.

IN THE YEARS SINCE MY FATHER'S DEATH, CHINA HAS LOST ITSELF.
THE WORDS DENOUNCING MY FATHER AS A *TRAITOR* STILL RING IN SOME OF OUR EARS.
BUT IT WAS MY FATHER WHO TOLD ME THAT THERE WAS LITTLE DIFFERENCE BETWEEN A HERO AND A SCAPEGOAT.
THAT'S WHY THERE ARE *STILL* SOME OF US WHO REMEMBER HIM HANGING IN PUBLIC HUMILIATION...A *HERO*.
A HERO WE *STILL* BELIEVE IN.

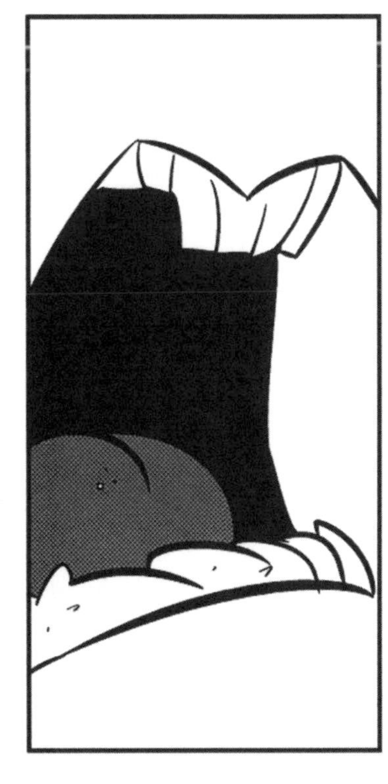

STORY: JEFF YANG
ART: KRISHNA M. SADASIVAM

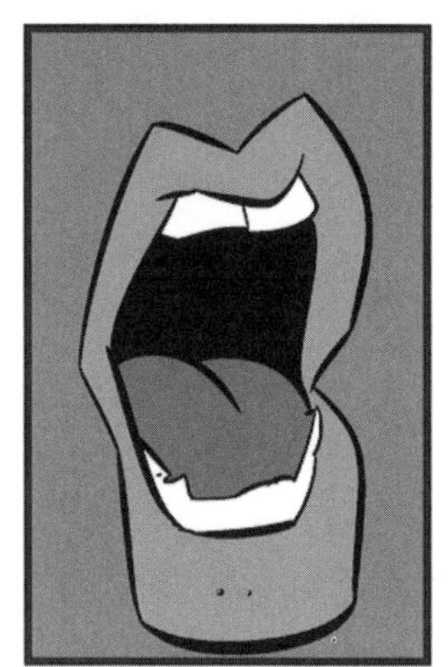

FAR AS AH'LL TAKE YOU BOYS. YOU C'N GRAB THE STAGE TO ST. LOU FROM HERE.
MAN ALIVE, MY BRUISES HAVE BRUISES.
MUSTA HIT EVERY ROCK AND FURROW 'TWEEN HERE 'N' TOMBSTONE.
THANK YOU FOR THE RIDE, SIR.

DON'T BE TOO QUICK T'THANK ME, CHINAMAN.
IF'N I WAS YOU, I'D JUMP TH' FIRST COACH OUT O' HERE AND NOT LOOK BACK.
WELC TO GOLD POP. 5(

STRANGE WAY OF MAKIN' PEOPLE FEEL WELCOME.
WELCOME TO GOLDFIELD POP. 505 503

JUSTICE CAN BE BRUTAL, JOHN-- IN MY LAND, AS MUCH AS YOURS.
LET'S HOPE THE TOWNSFOLK ARE FRIENDLIER THAN THIS DISPLAY SUGGESTS.
WE'RE SHORT ON FUNDS. IF WE PLAN ON MAKING OUR WAY EAST, WE'LL HAVE TO EARN OUR PASSAGE.

...THEN AGIN, THE CHINAMAN DONE GIVE ME MORE BUSINESS IN AN HOUR THAN I HAD ALL WEEK, SO I'LL DO YOU A CHRISTIAN TURN.

<I look in the mirror and what do I see? Five blasphemers, staring at me. KUM-SAU the brutish ZHI-LIK the sly BO-KWUN the shadow that rules from on high YI-YEUNG the stranger, NGAU-YUN the jade these five venoms would our world invade...>

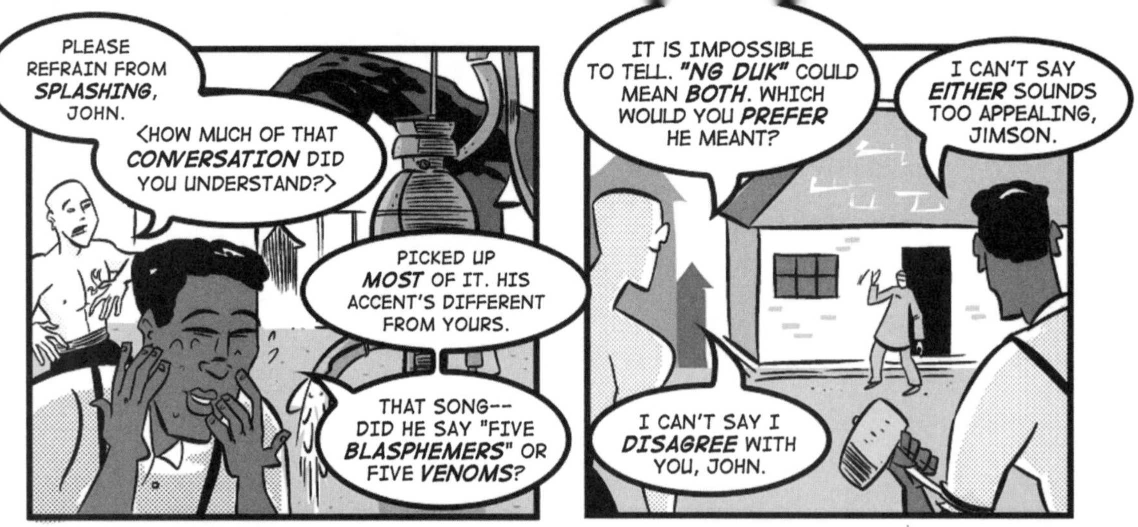
PLEASE REFRAIN FROM *SPLASHING*, JOHN.
<HOW MUCH OF THAT *CONVERSATION* DID YOU UNDERSTAND?>
PICKED UP *MOST* OF IT. HIS ACCENT'S DIFFERENT FROM YOURS.
THAT SONG--DID HE SAY "FIVE *BLASPHEMERS*" OR FIVE *VENOMS*?
IT IS IMPOSSIBLE TO TELL. *"NG DUK"* COULD MEAN *BOTH*. WHICH WOULD YOU *PREFER* HE MEANT?
I CAN'T SAY *EITHER* SOUNDS TOO APPEALING, JIMSON.
I CAN'T SAY I *DISAGREE* WITH YOU, JOHN.

WHA... *CHOLLIE??*
IN THIS PLACE, I ASK THAT YOU ADDRESS ME AS *"MASTER CHIA,"* MR. HENRY.
"CHOLLIE" IS A *CLOWN'S MASK* THAT ALLOWS ME TO KEEP WATCH ON THE *TOWNSFOLK* BELOW.
TO ENSURE THEY KEEP A PROPER DISTANCE--AND TO PROVIDE *REMINDERS* WHEN THEY FORGET.

REMINDERS. LIKE THE ONE WE SAW ENTERING TOWN.
JUST SO. WE USE OUR *GOLD* TO BUY OFF THE CURIOSITY OF THE FOREIGN DEVILS.
AND WHEN WE CANNOT *PURCHASE* DISCRETION--WE *ENFORCE* IT.
<TO HONOR YOU, *LORD OF FLAME*, WE OFFER THIS HUMBLE *GIFT*. IT SHOULD BE ENOUGH TO BUY YOU AND YOUR IMPETUOUS FRIEND *PASSAGE* ON TOMORROW'S EASTBOUND COACH.>
<TONIGHT, PLEASE SHARE OUR *HOSPITALITY*. I KNOW OF YOUR PEOPLE'S TASTE FOR *SPIRITS*; I INVITE YOU TO ENJOY SOME FINE *MAO TAI* WITH ME.
AND PERHAPS WE MIGHT PLAY SOME *CHESS*.>
<IT IS *WE* WHO ARE HONORED, MASTER CHIA.>

YOU AREN'T CURIOUS WHAT THESE GUYS ARE TRYING TO KEEP SECRET FROM US "FOREIGN DEVILS," JIMSON?
THEY ARE IN A LAND NOT THEIR OWN, SURROUNDED BY THOSE WHO WOULD TAKE THEIR LIVES AT ANY CHANCE FOR PROFIT, JOHN.
I...MISTRUST THE BRUTALITY OF THEIR MANNER. BUT I ALSO UNDERSTAND ITS ROOTS.
SO YOU'RE OFF TO DRINK WITH YOUR BUDDY, THEN.
IT SEEMS WISE TO GIVE FACE TO OUR HOST--AND PERHAPS LEARN SOMETHING ABOUT THE SITUATION IN THE PROCESS.
WILL YOU JOIN US, JOHN?
GONNA TURN IN. WE GOT AN EARLY START TOMORROW.
THE RIGHTEOUS AND HARMONIOUS FISTS HAVE FINALLY RISEN... TOO LATE FOR ANYTHING BUT GLORIOUS MARTYRDOM.
THE CHINESE BOXERS RISE IN REVOLT
YOU WERE A BOXER?
AYE, LIKE MANY IN THIS CAMP. BUT OUR LEADERS WERE WEAK AND WOULD NOT ACT WHEN THERE WAS TIME AND OPPORTUNITY.
WE HAD NO CHOICE BUT TO MOVE THE FIGHT SOMEWHERE NEW.
YET THE BATTLE SEEMS TO HAVE BEGUN IN CHINA.
I SPEAK OF A DIFFERENT BATTLE.
DO YOU PLAY CHESS, MASTER IFRIT? IT IS SAID THAT THE GAME WAS INVENTED BY ONE OF YOUR KIND.
NOT MY KIND--A DJINN, SATALAN THE GREAT.
THE TWISTY MINDS OF AIR ELEMENTALS ARE SUITED FOR SUCH PASTIMES.
BUT I KNOW THE RULES.
OR I THOUGHT I DID.
THIS IS UNLIKE ANY JEUNG KEI SET I'VE EVER SEEN.
THIS IS THE ORIGINAL VERSION.
IT IS QUITE HARD TO WIN IF YOU PLAY THE WHITE SIDE.
PERHAPS IMPOSSIBLE.

BETTER HOPE THAT *CHOLLIE* IS ON HIS FOURTH GLASS O' CHINESE *FIREWATER*, JOHN.

NGGGNHHHH!!!

OH LORD.

JOHN.

‹...KUM-SAU the brutish ZHI-LIK the sly BO-KWUN the shadow that rules from on high YI-HEUNG the stranger, NGAU-YUN the jade these five venoms would our world invade...›

FWAP

SPAK!

YOU THINK THAT I, A *WHITE LOTUS STYLE* MASTER, WOULD FEAR THAT CLUMSY WEAPON?

FEAR THIS THEN.

THOOM!
...laws, a hammer be the death of me...a hammer be the death of me....
WHAT HAVE YOU DONE, IFRIT??
THE MIRROR OF DIVINE IMMORTALS WAS THE SEAL BARRING THE FIVE VENOMS FROM OUR WORLD!
YOUR RASH ACT MEANS THAT THEIR CORRUPTION WILL BEGIN TO SPREAD. YOU HAVE DOOMED US ALL!

AH'M DOUBLIN' THE PRICE. THIS PLACE IS SET TO GO UP IN FLAMES. I GOT WOMENFOLK AND CHILDREN LININ' UP TO RIDE IF YOU WON'T PAY.
WE'LL PAY GOLD.

NEVER SEEN GOLD THIS COLOR-- BRIGHT RED, LIKE TO BE SOAKED IN BLOOD. BUT IT'S THE RIGHT WEIGHT.
GIT IN 'FORE I CHANGE MY MIND.

JOHN-- THIS IS ALL MY FAULT.
NO, JIMSON-- IT'S MINE. YOU GO LOOKING FOR TROUBLE, YOU GEN'RALLY FIND IT.

WE GOTTA FIND A WAY TO FIX THIS.
WE WILL, JOHN. EVEN IF IT TAKES A LIFETIME.

"And it did. My friend John Henry passed away barely three decades later--a blink of an eye to one such as me."

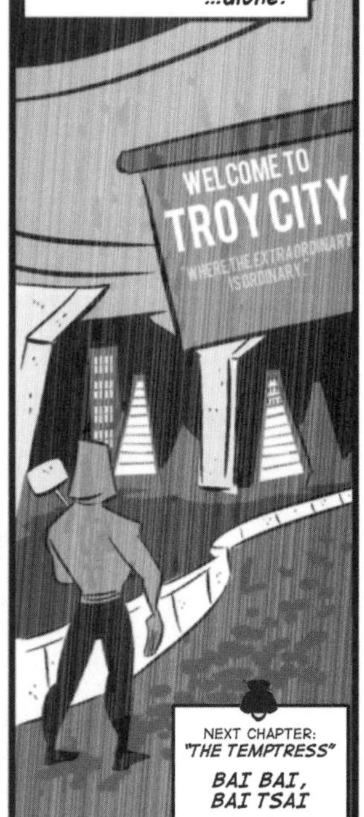
"Now I bear this burden... ...alone."
WELCOME TO TROY CITY
WHERE THE EXTRAORDINARY IS ORDINARY.
NEXT CHAPTER: "THE TEMPTRESS"
BAI BAI, BAI TSAI

MASTER TORTOISE & MASTER HARE

STORY: HOWARD WONG
ART: JAMIE NOGUCHI

MAKE WAY FOR MASTER HARE!
THE INVINCIBLE! UNBEATABLE!
天下無敵
QUICKEST KICK IN THE MARTIAL WORLD!

...THAT MASTER HARE, I HEARD HE ONCE WON A FIGHT IN THE BLINK OF AN EYE!
天下無敵

SPEED ISN'T EVERYTHING. THERE'S WISDOM. DISCIPLINE...
HE'D NEVER BEAT OUR MASTER TORTOISE!

...CAN'T BEAT A TORTOISE!?
A TORTOISE!? I'LL SHOW THEM!
IN HIS TRAVELS ACROSS THE EASTERN FOREST, MASTER HARE HAD BEATEN ALL OF THE LAND'S MOST POWERFUL WARRIORS.

FEATING THIS SHELL-BACKED SIMPLETON WOULD MOST BE TOO EASY FOR A FIGHTER OF HIS CALIBRE.
YOU! TORTOISE! ACCEPT MY CHALLENGE, AND LET ME PROVE TO YOU THAT I AM THE FASTEST FIST IN ALL OF EASTERN FOREST!

BOW BEFORE THE GLORY OF MASTER HARE!
NO NEED TO PROVE IT... I BELIEVE YOU. YOUR FISTS ARE CERTAINLY FASTER THAN MINE! NOW, WITH THAT SETTLED, WOULD YOU JOIN ME FOR SOME TEA?

MASTER HARE CONSIDERED MASTER TORTOISE'S INVITATION FOR TEA AND DECIDED...
I DON'T GET IT. WHO WON?
...TO ACCEPT HIS GRACIOUS OFFER.
WE CAN HAVE YOUR STUPID TEA—
AFTER I BEAT YOU SILLY!
HAAAAA!

BUT THE TEA WILL GET COLD...

...AND NO ONE LIKES...

...COLD TEA.

WOWEE! HE DIDN'T LAY A PAW ON HIM!
GO, MASTER TORTOISE!
MASTER HARE, THERE'S REALLY NO NEED FOR THIS.
I ALREADY AGREED THAT YOU HAVE THE FASTES FISTS.

ARE WE FINISHED?

YOU'LL BE FINISHED...
AFTER THIS!

ULTIMATE FLYING FIST OF FURRY!

AH, MY SPOON!
I'D BEEN WONDERING WHERE YOU'D WANDERED OFF TO.
BRAK!

MASTER TORTOISE WAS SO DELIGHTED BY MASTER HARE'S INCREDIBLE MOVE THAT HE ANNOUNCED MASTER HARE WAS THE GREATEST MARTIAL ARTIST HE'D EVER SEEN.
YOU WON! BUT WHY DID YOU SAY THAT HE'S THE GREATEST?
SINCE HE IS! HE'S SO POWERFUL THAT THE ONLY ONE WHO COULD EVER DEFEAT HIM IS... HIMSELF.

A TOAST TO MASTER HARE, THE FASTEST FIST IN THE EASTERN FOREST!
AND STILL UNBEATEN!
DRINK YOUR TEA BEFORE IT GETS COLD.
END

SHOWTIME

STORY & ART: BERNARD CHANG

NICE PASS, LEE!
GAME POINT UP!
LET'S GET ONE MORE STOP!

SCREEN LEFT, SAN! WATCH YOUR LEFT!
I SEE IT. STAY WITH YOUR MAN.

YO, CLEAR IT OUT. I'M TAKIN' THIS SUCKA TO DA HOLE!
GUESS YOU WEREN'T EXPECTING IT TO BE THIS CLOSE?
BROOKLYN
3

AND I GUESS YOU AIN'T EXPECTIN' DIS, CHINATOWN?

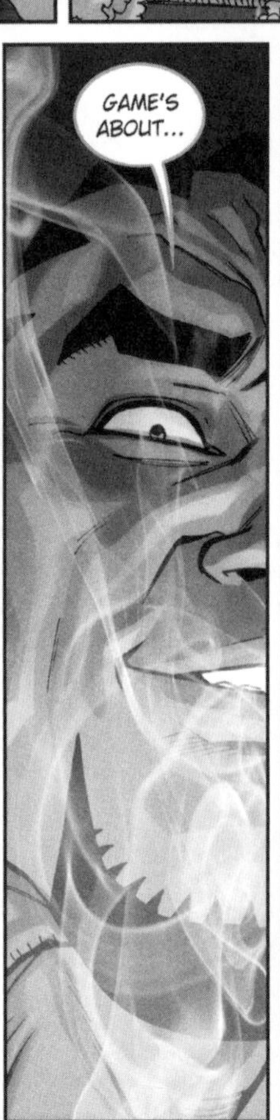
GAME'S ABOUT...

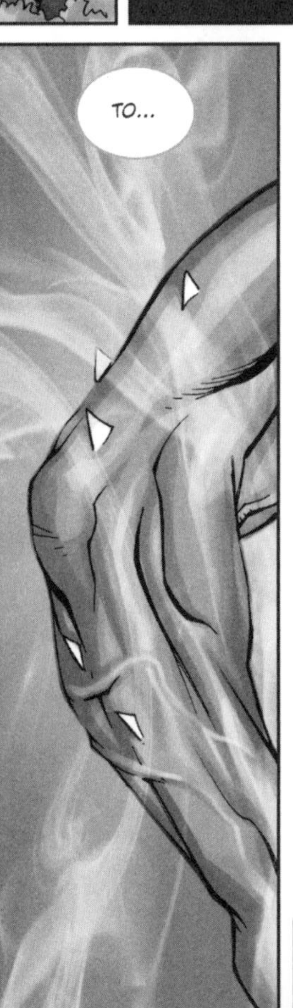
TO...

BE...
WHAT THE PHU--

OVA!

'ROUND THESE PARTS, THEY CALL ME...

...SWITCHBLADE!

RAAARRHHH!!!

OOOMMPHH!

OUTTA MY WAY, SUCKAS!

GAME!

TOO EASY!

WHO GOT NEXT?

YEEAH, SWITCH!

SAN! ARE YOU OKAY, BABY?

LET ME TAKE A LOOK AT THAT CUT.

HEY MAN, THAT WAS A *FOUL*!

YEAH, YOU GONNA CALL THAT?

I'M ALRIGHT. WHERE'S THE BALL?
COME ON, SAN. LET'S GO. I KNOW A GOOD RUN OUT IN CLINTON HILL. WE WON'T HAVE TO DEAL WITH KNUCKLEHEADS THERE.
HE COULDN'T HOLD YOU, SWITCH!
NO BLOOD NO FOUL, RIGHT, C-TOWN?
HAHA! NICE ONE, SWITCH!
BROOK
3
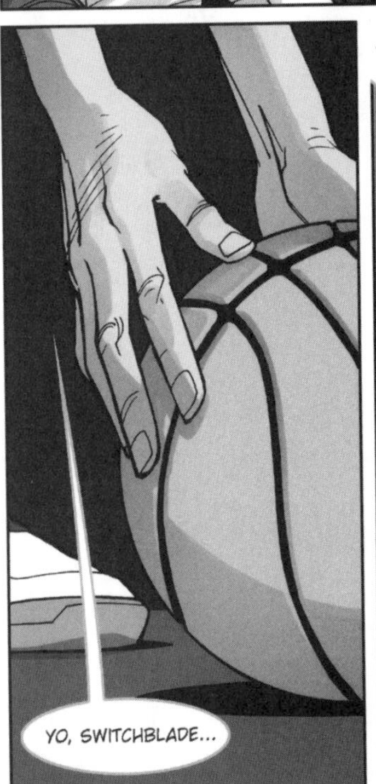
YO, SWITCHBLADE...

... RUN IT BACK. ONE ON ONE.
WHAH? YOU TIRED OF LIVIN'? BE HAPPY TO HELP YOU OUT.
THIS GUY THINKS HE'S JEREMY LIN OR SOMETHIN'?

GAME TO ELEVEN BY ONES.
OOKLYN
3

OH, AND BY THE WAY, YOU'RE NOT THE ONLY ONE AROUND HERE WITH A NICKNAME.
WHERE I'M FROM, THEY CALL ME...

...SHOWTIME!
BRO
FOR THE EXCITING CONCLUSION, SCAN THE QR CODE!
bernardchang.com/showtime.html

STORY: MICHAEL KANG & EDMUND LEE
ART: GLENN URIETA

EVERY DAY...
RODRIGUEZ 2357-65!
HERE.
ROH 4907-881!
PRESENT.
EVERY DAY BLEEDS INTO THE NEXT.
JUST LIKE JUVIE. TOO MANY SKINHEADS. TOO MANY 깜둥이*, TOO MANY CHOLOS.
* BLACK PEOPLE; LITERALLY, "EGGPLANTS"
AT LEAST NO ONE MESSES WITH ME ANYMORE. LEARNED TO KEEP A LOW PROFILE.
GIVES ME TIME TO THINK.
ROH. YOU'RE UP.
THIS IS THE GUY. PAROLE, OR BACK IN THE CAGE? HIS DECISION.
THIS GUY THINKS HE CAN CRACK ME.
OKAY. LET'S SEE WHAT WE GOT HERE. ARMED ROBBERY.
THREE YEARS IN JUVENILE DETENTION. TRANSFERRED HERE LAST MONTH AFTER YOUR 18TH BIRTHDAY.
HMM. STUYVESANT? GOOD SCHVOOL. LOOKS LIKE YOU DID PRETTY WELL, TOO.
THIS GUY DOESN'T KNOW JACK ABOUT KOREANS.

I WAS A STUPID KID. MADE A MISTAKE. DOING MY TIME. END OF STORY.
2008
ADJUSHI!
THE MISTAKE WAS BEING SLOPPY.
GRAB THE BAG! LET'S GO!

CAN YOU RELAX, HAN? YOU'RE MAKING ME NERVOUS. WE DID IT. IT'S DONE.
I'M COOL, I'M COOL. I'M GOOD, HYUNG.
I'M GONNA HOLD ON TO MOST OF IT FOR NOW. GOT IT? CAN'T GO OUT AND START FLASHING AROUND LIKE PIMPS OR THE ADJUSHIS'LL KNOW SOMETHING IS UP.
WHY DID I THINK YOU KNEW WHAT YOU WERE DOING, EUGENE?
JEENA...I MEAN, JEAN...HEY. WHAT'S UP?
SAT PREP.
"JEAN." YOU'LL ALWAYS BE JEENA TO ME.

WE LIVED TWO FLOORS AWAY FROM EACH OTHER. BUT IT MIGHT AS WELL HAVE BEEN THREE THOUSAND MILES.
WE USED TO BE SO TIGHT.
2002
WHEN I MOVED HERE, YOU WERE THE FIRST PERSON WHO TALKED TO ME.
YOU MADE ME FEEL NORMAL.
2004
YOU MADE ME FEEL LIKE IT WAS OKAY THAT MY DAD TOOK OFF.
ZZZZZ
WHEN I WAS TOO SCARED TO STAY UP WAITING FOR MY MOM BY MYSELF, YOU USED TO STAY UP WITH ME AND WATCH TV.
2008
EVEN THOUGH YOU HAD A REAL FAMILY ... I ALWAYS FELT LIKE YOU UNDERSTOOD.

WELCOME STUDENTS
STUYVESANT HIGH SCHOOL
THAT ALL CHANGED AFTER WE GOT TO STUY.
HEY, JEENA, WHAT LUNCH PERIOD YOU GET?
I TOLD YOU, DON'T CALL ME "JEENA"! IT'S JUST JEAN NOW.
SPANISH CLUB, STUDENT COUNCIL? THERE WAS NO WAY I COULD KEEP UP WITH YOU.
SO I STARTED HANGING WITH YOUR OLDER BROTHER, EUGENE.
YOU WANT RESPECT? YOU EARN IT. NOBODY'S GONNA JUST GIVE IT TO YOU.
HE HAD EVERYTHING I DIDN'T. CASH. CAR. GIRLS. WHATEVER HE SAID, I TOOK IT LIKE GOSPEL.
I HAD STUY COVERED, AND GOT INTO A FEW PRIVATE SCHOOL BATHROOMS DURING LUNCH.
HEY, JEENA--
SCREW HER. SHE'S HAD A STICK UP HER BUTT EVER SINCE MY DAD TOOK ONE OF HIS WAITRESSES TO A.C.
THE TRUTH IS, I THOUGHT HANGING WITH EUGENE WOULD GIVE ME AN EXCUSE TO BE AROUND YOU.

YOU CAN SIT HERE AND WAIT IT OUT LIKE YOU'RE IN SCHOOL AND THIS IS DETENTION, OR YOU CAN TALK TO ME, KID. BUT IT'S NOT HELPING YOU ANY TO CLAM UP.
I'VE SEEN THIS GANG LOYALTY B.S. A MILLION TIMES. I DON'T CARE WHO YOU'RE PROTECTING. OR WHY. BUT LET ME JUST ASK YOU THIS: HAS ANYONE FROM YOUR CREW EVER BOTHERED TO VISIT YOU?
SHUT THE HELL UP!
GUARD! GUARD!
AFTER FREAKING OUT ON THE SHRINK, YOU GOT A WEEK IN SOLITARY.
KP MEANS KOREAN POWER...
YOU'RE A GOOD EARNER, KID...
YOU'RE ONE OF US NOW...
NEVER SNITCH...
WE'LL ALWAYS HAVE YOUR BACK...
RESPECT...
I'M YOUR HYUNG...
FIVE YEARS MAX, THEN YOU'RE OUT...
LOYALTY IS ALL WE'VE GOT...
JEENA

OR MAYBE THE REAL MISTAKE WAS COMING BY YOUR PLACE THAT NIGHT TO BEGIN WITH.
YO, 계집*. JUST WHO I WAS LOOKING FOR. YOU'RE GONNA HELP ME OUT WITH A JOB.
I DON'T KNOW WHAT I WAS THINKING. IT WASN'T LIKE YOU'D'VE TALKED TO ME ANYWAY.
* FEMALE DOG
WE PICKING UP A NEW SHIPMENT?
NAW. FORGET THAT NICKEL-AND-DIME CRAP. THIS IS BIGGER.
GONNA BE REAL EASY. WHEN HE COMES ROLLING UP, JUST DISTRACT HIM. ASK HIM TO TAKE YOU TO ELMHURST OR SOMETHING. AND TAKE THIS.
IT'S JUST FOR SHOW. IN CASE HE CAUSES ANY PROBLEMS.
EUGENE HYUNG, I DON'T KNOW-
ARE YOU TALKING BACK TO ME?
NO, HYUNG.

ADJUSHI...
<WHADYA WANT, KID? SPIT IT OUT.>
<YOU DRIVE AND YOU'RE DEAD.>
<YOU'RE MAKING A BIG MISTAKE. DO YOU EVEN KNOW WHO YOU'RE SCREWING WITH?>
<SHUT UP, OLD MAN. I KNOW EXACTLY WHO YOU WORK FOR.>
<GRAB THE BAG! LET'S GO!>
F#*#-HAN! HAN!
야, 씨발!
BANG!
IT WENT OFF BY ACCIDENT. TOOK US ALL BY SURPRISE.
LET'S GO! LET'S GO!

ZZZZZZ
BAM BAM
OPEN UP! POLICE!
I'M OUT OF HERE. I CAN'T BE SEEN WITH YOU.
WHAT? BUT IT WAS YOUR IDEA!
THEY WON'T GIVE A CRAP ABOUT THAT. YOU PULLED THE TRIGGER. AND WHATEVER THE HELL YOU DO, HAN, REMEMBER: I'M YOUR HYUNG. SNITCH, AND YOU'RE DEAD.
<HAN? WHAT'S GOING ON?>
I DIDN'T DO IT!
JEENA! JEENA!
HE'S HEADED TO THE ROOF!
I SAW YOU THERE. LOOKING AT ME LIKE YOU HAD NO IDEA WHO I WAS. THEN AGAIN, I DIDN'T ANYMORE, EITHER.
JEENA. **I'M SORRY.**
MAKE ME RUN UP THESE STAIRS, PUNK? YOU'RE UNDER ARREST! FACE DOWN ON THE FLOOR! FACE DOWN!
PAROLE DENIED. THEY ALL THINK I TOOK THE FALL FOR SOME KINDA B.S. GANG LOYALTY. I DIDN'T PROTECT EUGENE BECAUSE HE WAS MY HYUNG. I DID IT FOR YOU, JEENA. EVEN IF YOU'VE FORGOTTEN ABOUT ME...IT WAS WORTH IT.
RIGHT?
END

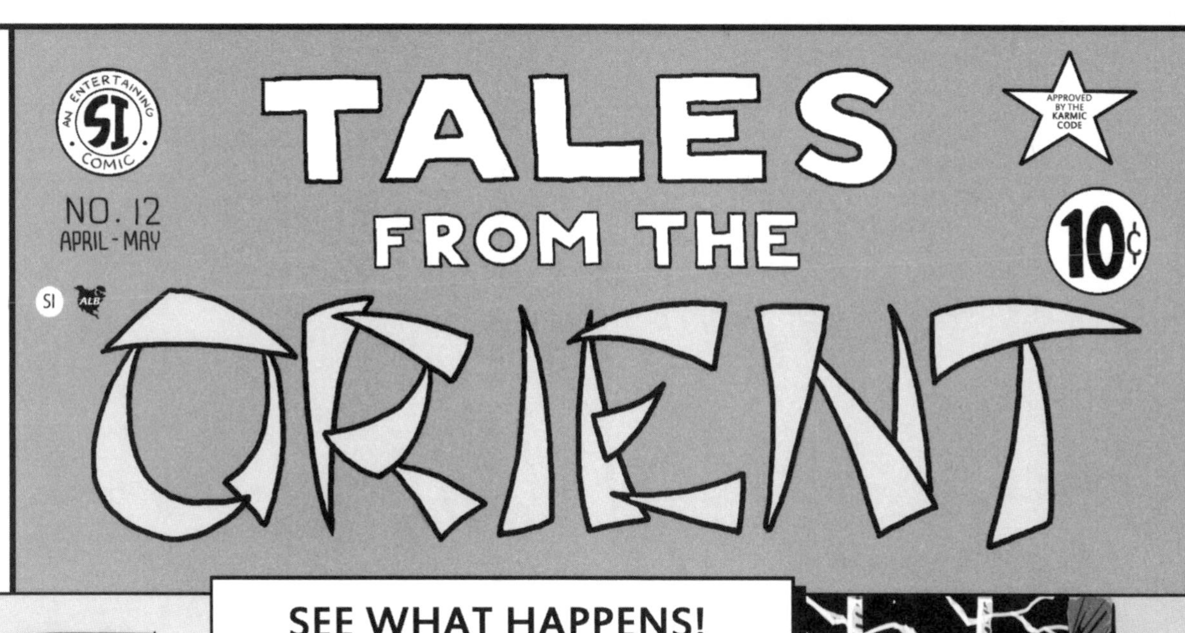

CLEAN GETAWAY

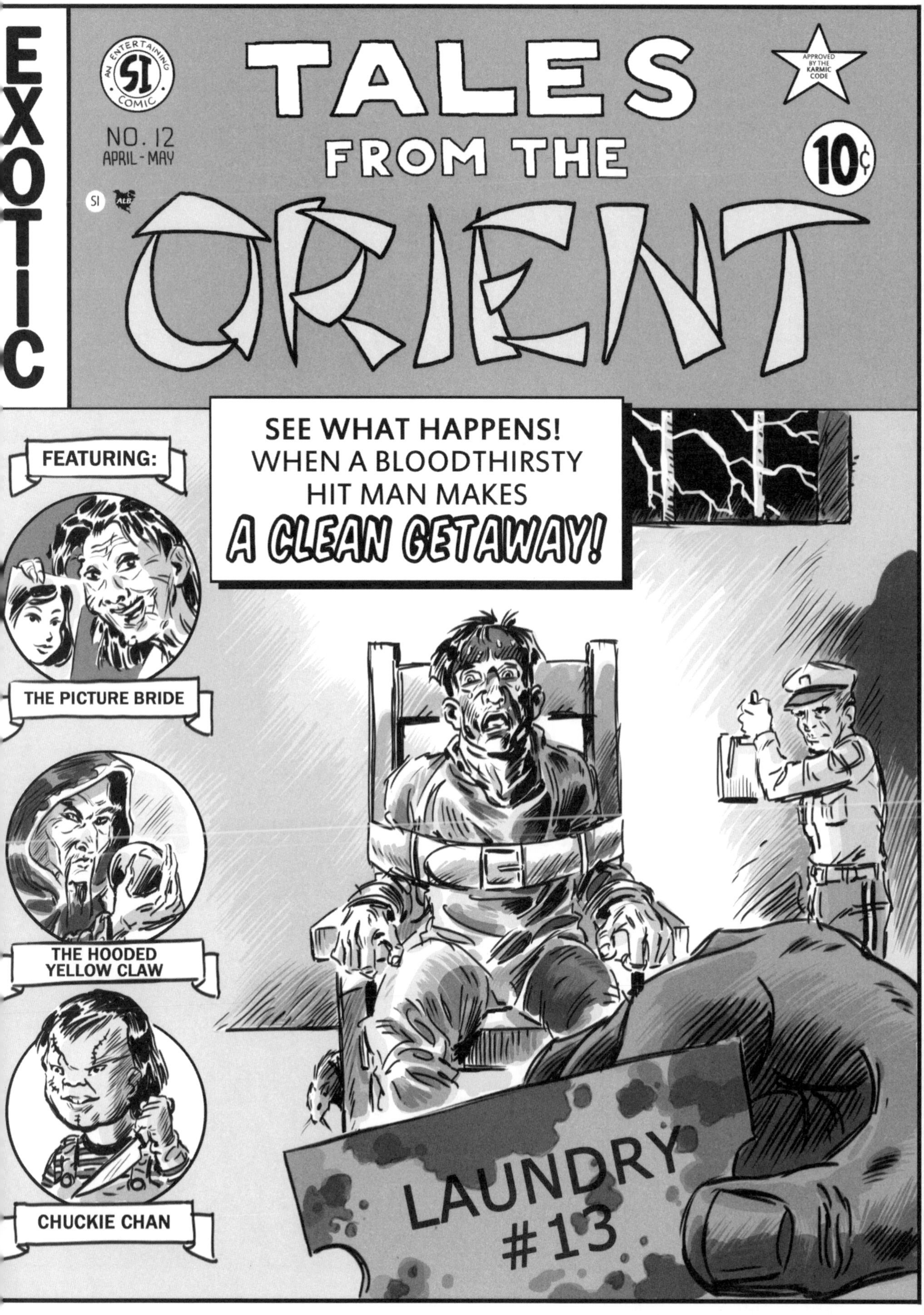

STORY: JAMIE FORD
ART: A.L. BAROZA

MOB HITMAN SQUEAKY MORENO KNOWS WHERE TO GO TO COME CLEAN.
BLOOD-STAINS VERY BAD THIS TIME.
DON'T BOTHER ME WITH THE DETAILS. JUST MAKEE CLEAN, CHOP CHOP!
YOU PAY EXTRA!

BUT AT CHING'S LAUNDRY, IT DOESN'T PAY TO PRESS THE ISSUE.
LAU
I BEEN COMIN' HERE FOR YEARS! WHADDAYA MEAN I CAN'T GET MY SUIT IF I DON'T GOT MY TICKET?
NO TICKEE!
NO SHIRTEE!

I WANT MY STUFF AND I WANT IT NOW! AND I'LL TAKE ALL THE MONEY WHILE I'M AT IT!
YOU'LL BE SORRY, MR. MORENO.
VERY SORRY.

FORGET IT, FLATFOOT! YOU CAN'T PROVE A THING!
YOU KNOW THE LOWER WEST SIDE MASSACRE?

WE FOUND THIS AT THE CRIME SCENE! YOU'RE GONNA FRY THIS TIME, SQUEAKY!
MORENC

I GUESS YOU COULD SAY THIS STORY HAD A WRINKLE SQUEAKY DIDN'T EXPECT!
AND NOW, IT'S TIME FOR A... SHOCKING CONCLUSION! HAHAHA!
NOOOO!
EN

BAI BAI, BAI TSAI

THE TEMPTRESS

WELCOME TO
Harmonica
BIG FUN DAY!
THE EXTRAORDINARY OFFSPRING* OF SUBURBAN HEROES PORTIA ("PORTAL") AND PRESTON ("PRESTO CHANGE-O") CHANG--VAL (A.K.A. "MAGICAL GIRL"), VERNON (A.K.A. "SUPER-DEFORMED") AND VIVVIE (A.K.A. "HELL KITTY")--ARRIVE AT TROY CITY PARK FOR A SPECIAL DAY OF KIDTASTIC FUN!
C'MON, VAL, THIS IS GREAT!
LOOK, VIVVIE, THE FRONT-PORTUGEESE!
I CAN'T BELIEVE I'M MISSING A CHESS MATCH FOR THIS.
YAY!
*AS SEEN IN "A DAY AT COSTUMECO," SECRET IDENTITIES FANS!

DON'T BE SUCH A SOURPUSS, SIS. THIS IS A TOTALLY ENTER-CATIONAL EVENT!
"LIKE THE INSTRUMENT, HARMONICA IS ABOUT FUN AND WONDER AND LEARNING THROUGH PLAY."
CORRECTION. LIKE THE INSTRUMENT, HARMONICA BLOWS. THEIR SHOWS ARE DUMB, INFANTILIZING, AND FULL OF GROSS JOKES ABOUT BODILY FUNCTIONS.
SLUDGEBLOB!!!
TRANSFORM!
POOOOT!

chica the seeker!
POOOOT!
MORPH!
mint's hints!
CHANGE!
Abbastar
POOOOT!
ALTER!
SHOWOFF.

STORY: JEFF YANG
ART: MARTIN HSU & SOPHIA LIN

REEREE, OVER THERE, OVER THERE!

Harmonica

C'MON, GUYS, LET'S GO GO GO!

THWOCK!

SKA-WHACK!
EEK!

AAAHH!

IS THIS REALLY APPROPRIATE FOR KINDERGARTNERS?
UH, VAL, I THINK SOMETHING'S HAPPENING.

COME AND MEET MY GOOD FRIENDS
THEY'RE ALL READY TO SLAY
AND NOW THAT WE'RE HERE
YOU'D BETTER START TO PRAY

I'D LIKE TO GIVE MY FRIENDS A TASTY TREAT TO EAT
AND WHEN THEY LOOK AT YOU FOLK WHAT THEY'RE SEEING IS FRESH MEEEEAAAT...
C'MON, GUYS, LET'S KILL KILL KILL!
SKA-KOW!
ROAAARR
DON'T JUST STAND THERE, IDIOT--GET VIVVIE OUT OF HERE!
Finally, mistress! Ugh, what are you wearing? My stars and rainbows (choke)...capri pants?
LESS MOUTH, MORE MAGIC, WAND.
"JUSTICE IS MY SWORD, AND LOVE IS MY SHIELD..."
I AM THE BEAUTIFUL WARRIOR WHO...
GAH! FINISH CHANGING ME, WAND!
Not until you complete the spell and strike four cute magical poses.
And has this monkey ever been washed?
HROOOMM?

KLUDDDD!

WELL, IF IT ISN'T HARMON ICKES *HIMSELF*. I SHOULD'VE KNOWN YOU'D GET OFF ON THIS, *SCUM*.
NO, WAIT, I CAN *EXPLAIN*....

NOO!

...LYCHEE?

VIVVIE...*RUN*! I CAN *TAKE* THIS GUY!

BOBO! IGNORE THE *BRAT*--GET ME THAT *PANDA!*
SMOOTH *MOVE*, EX-LAX.
BUDDUDDA BUDDUDDA
???
BUDDUDDA BUDDUDDA

PLEASE, NO!

COME ON, BOBO, TAI-REN! GEN WO LAI! LET'S GO GO GO!
SPLORT

WAND, LIGHT UP.
Would it kill you to ask nicely, mistress?
LIGHT UP OR I'LL USE YOU TO ROAST MARSHMALLOWS.

...We appear to have different definitions of "nice."
AGGGH! I'VE GONE BLIND!

THWOK
LISTEN, STICK, YOU MAY NOT BE ABLE TO CHANGE ME FORWARD, BUT YOU SHOULD AT LEAST BE ABLE TO CHANGE ME BACK, RIGHT?
As you wish, mistress. You do realize I'm not a melee weapon, don't you?

THIS IS...THE SET OF BAI BAI, BAI TSAI.
BUT THE SHOW'S STILL RUNNING. WHY DOES IT LOOK SO... ABANDONED?

FOOLS!
PRODUCTION ON BAI BAI, BAI TSAI ENDED A DECADE AGO...AFTER HARMONICA BOOKED ENOUGH EPISODES TO RERUN THEM INDEFINITELY.

WOW. I NEVER EVEN NOTICED. I MEAN, I GUESS EVERY EPISODE IS PRETTY MUCH THE SAME.

GROARRR

THAT'S EXACTLY WHAT ICKES AND HIS THUGS WANTED YOU TO THINK. SO THEY COULD USE US, DRAIN US OF OUR INNOCENCE--AND THEN THROW US AWAY.

ARE YOU... (GULP) ARE YOU BAI-TSAI?

I WAS, ONCE.
NOW...I AM VENGEANCE.

"WHEN CHICA THE SEEKER TURNED 16, SHE WAS TOLD HER WORK VISA WOULDN'T BE RENEWED."
"SHE WAS DEPORTED, AND DIED TRYING TO COME BACK ACROSS THE BORDER."

"THE BUGBRATS ENDED UP IN JUVIE."

"THE PEPPERPUNCH GIRLS ARE STILL 'PERFORMING' AS THE PEPPERPUNCH GIRLS."

"AND THEN THERE'S ME. HARMON ICKES TOOK A SPECIAL INTEREST IN ME. HE TOLD ME I MIGHT 'GRADUATE' TO A TWEEN SHOW..."
"...IF I AGREED TO BE 'NICE' TO HIM."

"MY PO-PO SAVED ME, JUST IN TIME."
TOUCH HER AGAIN, ICKES, AND YOUR CROTCH IS NEXT.
KRUMP

SIT WITH ME, CHILD.

"PO-PO'S FATHER HAD BEEN A MINER IN A SMALL TOWN IN ARIZONA DURING THE GOLD RUSH. HE'D TAUGHT HER HOW TO FIGHT. HOW TO SURVIVE."

"BUT THERE WAS TROUBLE WHEN SHE BECAME PREGNANT WITH MY MOTHER. SHE KNEW SHE HAD TO ESCAPE. FORTUNATELY, HER FATHER HAD TOLD HER THE LOCATION OF AN UNIMAGINABLE TREASURE, HIDDEN DEEP UNDERGROUND."

"MY GREAT-GRANDFATHER LOST HIS LIFE IN A VIOLENT RIOT. AS THE TOWN WHERE THEY LIVED BURNED, PO-PO TRADED THE SECRET OF THE TREASURE TO A GERMAN MERCHANT IN EXCHANGE FOR SAFE PASSAGE BACK EAST. THAT WAS TIM ICKES...HARMON'S FATHER."
"TYCOON" TIM ICKES DISCOVERS LOST CACHE OF GOLD!
HEADING BACK EAST RICHER THAN MIDAS
BLOODY MASSACRE IN GOLDFIELD
67 CHINAMEN MURDERED IN ONE NIGHT — A NEW RECORD

"HE USED THE GOLD TO BUILD AN EMPIRE, AND PROMISED PO-PO THAT HE'D TAKE CARE OF HER AND HER DESCENDANTS FOREVER.
BUT THAT GOLD...IT STANK OF EVIL. WHEN HARMON CAME OF AGE, TIM ICKES DIED IN A MYSTERIOUS ACCIDENT. MY PARENTS WERE LOST TRYING TO SAVE HIM."
"HARMON INHERITED EVERYTHING. I ALWAYS SUSPECTED HE WAS SOMEHOW TO BLAME."

"HARMON TOOK HIS HUMILIATION AT PO-PO'S HANDS POORLY."

"SHE SACRIFICED HERSELF FOR ME."

"BUT THOUGH MY BODY SURVIVED, MY HEART WAS KILLED THAT NIGHT."

"I WANTED REVENGE. AND FOR THAT... I NEEDED MY FRIENDS."

BANG
"NOT ALL OF THEM MADE IT."

I HAD A MOMENT OF WEAKNESS WHEN I SAW YOU IN THAT PANDA FORM, BOY. LYCHEE USED TO MAKE MY HEART FEEL SUPER-HAPPY.
BUT LIFE GOES ON. FOR ME, ANYWAY. FOR YOU? NOT SO MUCH.

REE-REE...
NOT SO FAST.
GRARGHH
HROOMM
VIVVIE! MOM!

HOW'D YOU FIND US, MOM?
I JUST TUNED INTO YOUR WAND'S INTENSE FEELINGS OF SULKINESS AND DISSATISFACTION. IT'S A MOM THING.

BECOME!

RARRH

OK, WAND, I ADMIT IT. I'VE BEEN A LITTLE HARD ON YOU LATELY. BYGONES?
TIME TO PRINCESS UP, WAND.

Hmff. Every time you're in a tough spot, you expect me to come running back to you like I'm some kind of--
--HOT DAMN.

"JUSTICE IS MY SWORD AND LOVE IS MY SHIELD..."
"I AM THE BEAUTIFUL WARRIOR WHO BRINGS LIGHT TO THE DARKNESS

PRETTY SUPER
schoolgirl valentine!

UM, A LITTLE HELP HERE? OW!

--SORT OF BUSY!
NOT A MELEE WEAPON
NOT A MELEE WEAPON
NOT A MELEE WEAPON

HAAAALP

HEY, VERN! YOU KNOW WHAT YOUR PROBLEM IS? YOU FIGHT LIKE A GRANDMOTHER.

TRANSMOGRIFY!

NOOOOOO!!!!

SKA-WHACK!
SKA-KOW!

UNGGHH!

VAL--I'M SENSING THERE'S SOMETHING ODD ABOUT THAT PIECE OF GLASS.
A "MOM THING" AGAIN?

LOVE-LOVE HEART BEAM!
NOOOOOOOO!!

SOMEHOW, I GET THE FEELING THIS ISN'T OVER.
YOU KNOW, VAL, FOR THE RECORD, BOTH OF YOUR GRANDMOTHERS WERE PRETTY BADASS.

WHY DO YOU STILL HAVE THAT THING?
LET'S JUST CALL IT A SOUVENIR.
NEXT CHAPTER: "THE BRAIN"
HIDE & SIKH

CHING SHIH: QUEEN OF PIRATES

STORY: NATALIE KIM
ART: ROBIN HA

OUTH CHINA SEA, 1805. A BLOODY FIGHT CONTINUES DEEP NTO THE NIGHT ON A PIRATE SHIP, *THE GODDESS OF THE SEA.*

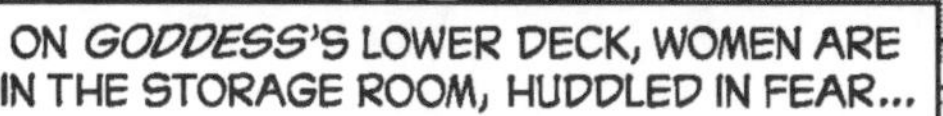

ON *GODDESS*'S LOWER DECK, WOMEN ARE IN THE STORAGE ROOM, HUDDLED IN FEAR...

...EXCEPT FOR ONE.
LET ME OUT! I NEED TO PEE!
BAM BAM

OUTSIDE OF THE STORAGE ROOM...
YI WANTS YOU DOWN HERE.

USELESS IDIOT.
JUST BE QUIET UNTIL THE FIGHTING ENDS!

...YI.

FOUR YEARS EARLIER...

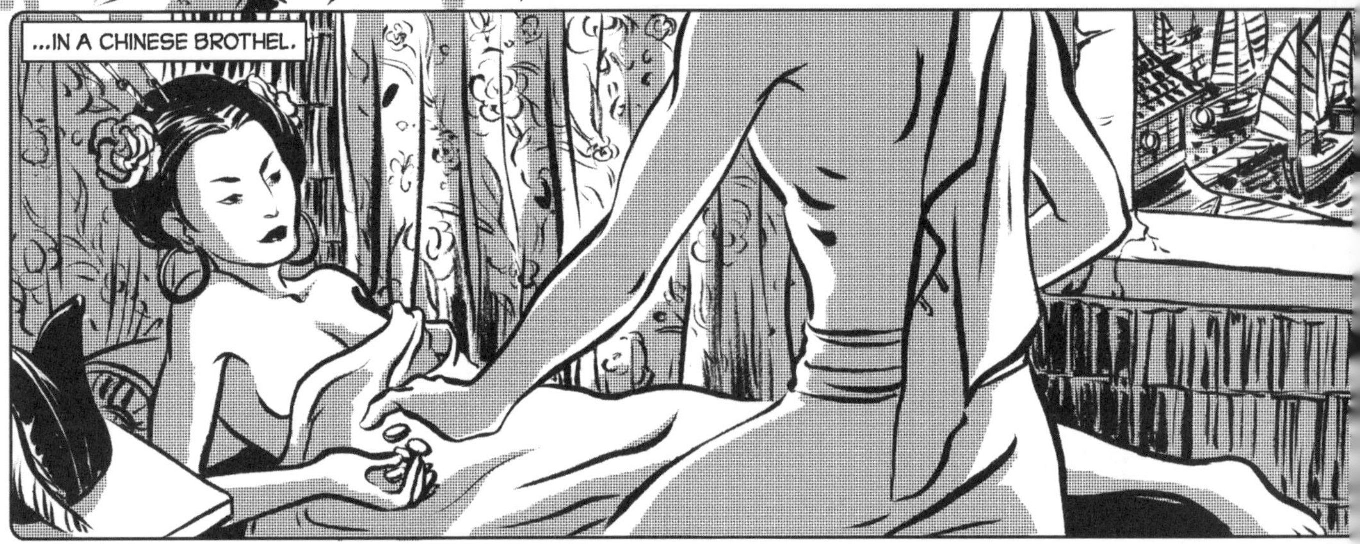
...IN A CHINESE BROTHEL.

I'LL MISS YOU...
I TOLD YOU, YOU CAN'T DO THAT.

EVEN THOUGH THIS COULD BE THE LAST TIME YOU EVER SEE ME? I SAIL IN AN HOUR. THE SEA IS DANGEROUS; I MIGHT NOT RETURN.

I SUPPOSE YOU DON'T CARE.
WAIT—I WILL WALK OUT WITH YOU.

I CAN'T BE APART FROM YOU ANY LONGER.
WHAT CAN WE DO? YOU'RE THE CAPTAIN OF THE RED FLEET, AND YOU SAIL IN AN HOUR.

COME WITH ME.
AND LIVE ON A PIRATE SHIP? I CAN EARN A LIVING HERE!

I'M WAITING FOR YOU, CHING!
THEN I SUPPOSE THIS IS GOOD-BYE.

FINE. I'LL GO.

BUT YOU'LL BE MY HUSBAND--AND YOU'LL DO AS I SAY.

THE RED FLEET SAILS NOW.
YES, MA'AM!
THIEF! KIDNAPPER! BRING THAT WOMAN BACK!
YAH! CHING! WHERE DO YOU THINK YOU'RE GOING?!

1805, THE STORAGE ROOM OF GODDESS OF THE SEA.
WOOOOO
YI!
HYAAAA
KRAASH
Hehe...

SLIP
SWOOSH

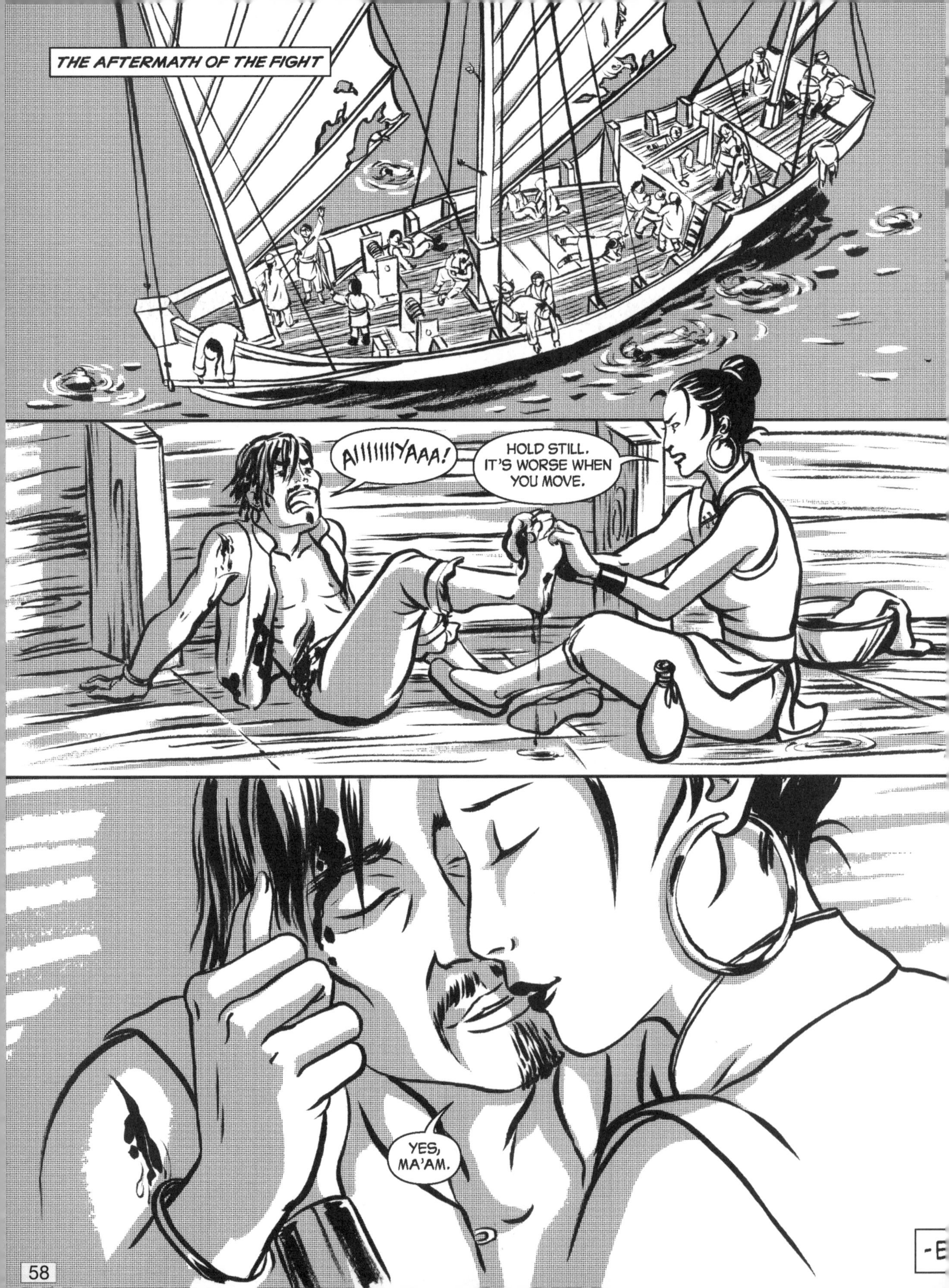
THE AFTERMATH OF THE FIGHT
AIIIIIIIYAAA!
HOLD STILL. IT'S WORSE WHEN YOU MOVE.
YES, MA'AM.
-E

THE REGRETS WE TALK ABOUT

STORY & ART: FRED CHAO

Growing up, I listened to a lot of hip hop -- Pharcyde, Brand Nubian, A Tribe Called Quest.

Because I'm **RAWR RAWR** like a ***dungeon*** dragon!

CHANGE YOUR LITTLE DRAWERS 'CUZ YOUR **PANTS** ARE SAGGIN'!

I don't so much revisit those old albums, but there are two songs I still listen to more often than I care to admit.

Both have two people rapping back and forth -- a dialogue.

SEX PACKETS

digital undergro

In "Packet Man," a dealer tries to sell Humpty a new kind of drug, one that puts you into the sexual fantasy described on the packaging.

POSITIVE K

THE SKILLS DAT PAY DA BILLS

In "I Got A Man," Positive K relentlessly hits on a girl who says she's got a boyfriend, to which K keeps responding, "What's your man got to do with me?"

Along with pithy, fun dialogue, both songs have characters who slightly change, which I really liked. Usually songs are written after an emotional realization; rarely do we see the character change ***during*** a song.

When I was just out of college I lived in this great party apartment.

I remember one party where I met this girl.
Hey, Emily. I'm Fred.
She was pretty hot and we got along right away.

We pretty much talked nonstop...
Are you kidding? *Back To The Future 3* is amazing!
I mean, Flea rocks out to "The Power of Love!"

Why ***not*** Papa Smurf? All the others were losers.
It was easy for you--there was only Smurfette.
...exchanging flirty touches...

...getting down on the dance floor...
You talk about Snoop all night, but here you are singing every word of "Take On Me."

...onto the roof, with everyone else smoking up and taking in the dawn.

The sunrise was, of course, beautiful.

I turned to kiss her and, like a record scratch, she interrupted my move with:
Um, I have a boyfriend.

To which I replied, borrowing the amazingly poetic words of Positive K:
What's your man got to do with me?

Yeah, right. I **wish** I was that smooth.
In reality, I backed off, probably saying something along the lines of:
Oh, okay. Um, that's cool.
I've told this story before, saying my biggest regret was **not** reciting those lyrics **at that moment**--the missed opportunity of a lifetime.
Though right now, writing this down, I see this is obviously a lie. My **biggest** regret?

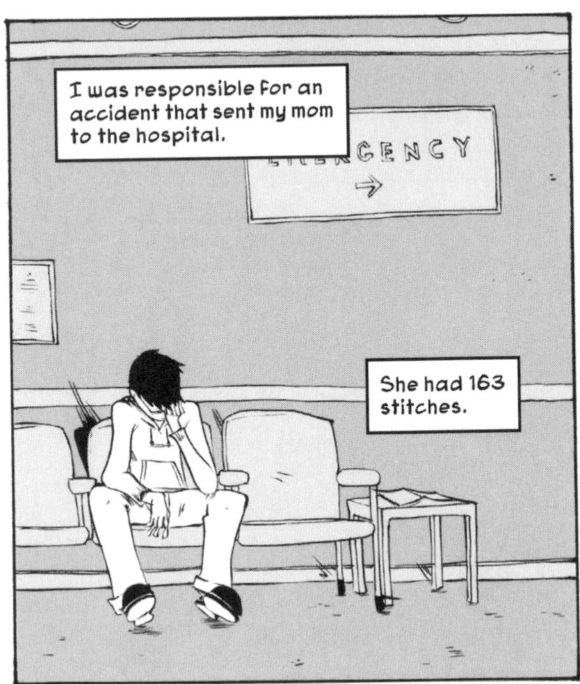
I was responsible for an accident that sent my mom to the hospital.
She had 163 stitches.

I once slammed a door on my little sister's fingers. Her fingernail fell off and she had to soak her fingertip in medicine every night.
She cried loudly.

I regret not calling my best friend more often. Not that we're not friends, but I think we both feel the distance that's grown between us.

I missed my grandmother's funeral.

But on the rooftop with that girl, I ***know*** I could have recognized it as a lighter moment while still ***in*** the moment.

Hell, if I had, we might have made out a little.

I don't know--most likely we still would have just stood there awkwardly.

But reciting those words Positive K once rapped might have at least changed the context of this memory.

Because instead of a story about regret, I'd love for this to be just another stupid story I like to tell.

END

HEROES WITHOUT A COUNTRY: TOKYO ROSE

STORY: DANIEL JAI LEE
ART: DAFU YU

"HISTORY IS A TRICKY THING..."
"...ESPECIALLY IF YOU *DON'T* OFFICIALLY EXIST."
"NO ONE KNOWS MY REAL NAME."
"NO ONE KNOWS MY REAL FACE."
"I HAVE A *SCAR* ON MY CHEEK. GOT IT FROM A BIKE ACCIDENT WHEN I WAS A KID."
"BUT YOU'D *NEVER* KNOW THAT EITHER."
"THAT'S BECAUSE OF THE '*SECRET SURPRISE*' GOD PUT IN MY LITTLE BOX OF CRACKER JACKS."
"WHEN YOU LOOK AT ME, I BECOME WHAT YOU WANT TO SEE: THE MOST BEAUTIFUL GIRL IN THE WORLD. YOUR FEMALE FANTASY. YOUR ASIAN *DREAM GIRL*."
"THAT'S MY SPECIAL POWER. MY GIFT. *MY CURSE*."
"THEY CALL ME '*TOKYO ROSE*'..."
BERLIN, GERMANY. 1943
"...AND TONIGHT IS GOING TO BE A LONG NIGHT."

HIROSHIMA, JAPAN. 1941
"IT ALL STARTED HERE--TWO YEARS AGO. WHEN MY GRANDMOTHER FELL ILL, I MOVED FROM CALIFORNIA TO JAPAN TO TAKE CARE OF HER."
"AFTER BAA-CHAN RECOVERED, I WAS ALL SET TO HEAD BACK, WHEN..."

PEARL HARBOR, HAWAII. 1941
"...WELL, LET'S JUST SAY THINGS GOT COMPLICATED."

"MY OWN COUNTRY *REFUSED* TO LET ME GO BACK HOME."

"THEY TOLD ME THE ONLY WAY I COULD WIN BACK THEIR TRUST WAS TO PUT MY '*SECRET SURPRISE*' TO WORK..."
"...AS AN AGENT FOR THE U.S. ARMY'S METAHUMAN COVERT OPS DIVISION, THE *XSF*."

"MY ASSIGNMENT LED TO ME HOSTING A SHOW ON RADIO TOKYO. THAT'S WHERE I GOT MY CODE NAME. AND WHERE I BECAME THE MOST NOTORIOUS *PROPAGANDA TOOL* OF THE PACIFIC WAR."
ON AIR

"THE JAPANESE USED MY BROADCASTS TO *DEMORALIZE* AMERICAN G.I.S--MAKING ME READ STORIES OF U.S. SOLDIERS WHO DIED IN BATTLE..."
"...OF UNFAITHFUL WIVES AND GIRLFRIENDS BACK HOME."

"MEANWHILE, I WAS USING THEM TO SEND *CODED MESSAGES* TO OUR BOYS BACK HOME. TROOP MOVEMENTS. SUPPLY-CHAIN INTEL. THE LOCATIONS OF KEY STRATEGIC ASSETS."
ANYTHING I COULD *SWEET-TALK* OUT OF THE DRONES AT THE IMPERIAL INFORMATION MINISTRY--WHICH, GIVEN MY *POWERS*, WAS PRETTY MUCH ANYTHING I WANTED.

BERLIN, GERMANY. 1943.
HOW YOU DOING, *ROSIE?*
LONG TIME NO SEE...

"CAPTAIN MATT KIM, LEADER OF THE SUNSET SQUAD AND MY XSF OPERATOR."
JUST LIKE OLD TIMES, CAPTAIN.

WELCOME TO GERMANY, ROSE. I'M SURE YOU'RE WONDERING WHY WE HAD YOU ACCEPT THE INVITATION TO APPEAR AT TOMORROW'S *REICHSFEIER*. WELL, I'LL MAKE IT QUICK: THE KRAUTS HAVE MADE A BREAKTHROUGH.
IT'S A GAME-CHANGER. MAYBE A *GAME-ENDER.* AND OUR INTEL SAYS THE GALA IS A COVER FOR THE TRANSFER OF PLANS FOR *"PROJECT TERMINUS"*...
...FROM HITLER'S EXOTIC *RESEARCH LAB* TO THEIR MAJOR WEAPONS SUPPLIER FRIED. KRUPP AG ESSEN.
YOUR MISSION IS TO *INTERCEPT* THOSE DOCUMENTS.

NOTHING I HAVEN'T HANDLED BEFORE.
THIS IS DIFFERENT. THIS IS THE WHOLE WAR. YOU SUCCEED, *WE WIN.* YOU FAIL, WE LOSE.
WHICH IS WHY, THIS TIME, WE'RE NOT SENDING YOU IN ALONE. YOU HAVE AN *ESCORT.* AND HE'S DUE TO ARRIVE RIGHT ABOUT...

...NOW.

NOT HIM. ABSOLUTELY NOT.
ENCHANTED AS ALWAYS, ROSITA.
COULD YOU HAVE PICKED A *TELEPORTER* WHO HASN'T ASKED ME OUT A MILLION TIMES?

IT IS HARDLY MY FAULT THAT YOU ARE SO BEAUTIFUL.
SAYS YOU...AND EVERYONE ELSE.

I DON'T NEED HIM TO SNEAK ME IN. I'VE GOT AN INVITATION.
HE'S NOT THERE TO GET YOU IN. HE'S THERE TO GET YOU AND THE DOCUMENTS *OUT*. FAST.
SO, IT IS A DATE?

"THAT'S WHY I'M HERE IN NAZI CENTRAL WITH LOVERBOY IN TOW. THE GERMAN MINISTRY OF INFORMATION SPONSORED THIS GALA."
"I'M HERE AS THE AXIS'S ALLY FROM THE PACIFIC RIM."
"THE SUPERSTARS OF AXIS PROPAGANDA. LORD HAW HAW. AXIS SALLY. AND THE PUPPETEER HIMSELF, JOSEPH GOEBBELS, THE NAZI MINISTER OF PROPAGANDA."
AH, SO WELL NAMED--YOU ARE INDEED AS LOVELY AS A ROSE. WHAT A PLEASURE IT IS TO MEET YOU IN PERSON! PLEASE, MAKE SURE NOT TO LEAVE TOO EARLY; WE HAVE A SURPRISE FOR YOU AND OUR OTHER HONORED GUESTS.
"A SURPRISE? THAT CAN'T BE GOOD. WE'D BETTER DO THIS QUICK."
SST, ROSITA: TARGET SIGHTED.
KRUPP
THAT WAS FUN. WHAT SHALL WE DO ON OUR NEXT DATE?
THIS WAS NOT A DATE, D'AQUINO. NOW GET US THE HELL--
FRAULEIN ROSE! AH, PLEASE, SO NOT LEAVE BEFORE YOU MEET OUR SURPRISE GUEST OF HONOR!

DER FÜHRER!
"...THIS PARTY JUST GOT A LOT MORE INTERESTING."
PLEASE COME WITH ME, AND I SHALL INTRODUCE YOU IN PRIVATE.
DER FÜHRER HAS LONG WISHED TO MEET YOU IN PERSON, FRAULEIN ROSE, AS HE HAS HEARD TALES OF YOUR AMAZING BEAUTY--ALL QUITE TRUE.
"AS I SAID BEFORE, HISTORY IS A TRICKY THING... AND SOMETIMES IT THROWS YOU A CURVEBALL."
FELIPE, THE MISSION'S CHANGED.
YOU AREN'T GOING TO DO WHAT I THINK YOU'RE GOING TO DO.
WHY NOT? WE CAN END THE WAR-- RIGHT HERE, RIGHT NOW.
PLEASE...WE CAN'T AFFORD TO LOSE THESE DOCUMENTS.
AND I, WELL, I CANNOT AFFORD TO LOSE YOU.
LET ME TELEPORT US OUT OF HERE RIGHT NOW.
YOU CAN'T TAKE ME IF MY MIND WON'T LET YOU. AND I'M NOT LEAVING--NOT WITH A CHANCE LIKE THIS.
IF YOU ARE SO CERTAIN YOU MUST DO THIS...
...THEN I MUST TAKE MY LEAVE OF YOU, KAIBIG-IBIG.
KEEP ME IN YOUR MIND UNTIL YOU SEE ME NEXT.
"COWARD. NEVER TRUST A MAN WHO CAN VANISH INTO THIN AIR."
I DON'T NEED HIM. I CAN DO THIS MYSELF.
TONIGHT, I KILL ADOLF HITLER.

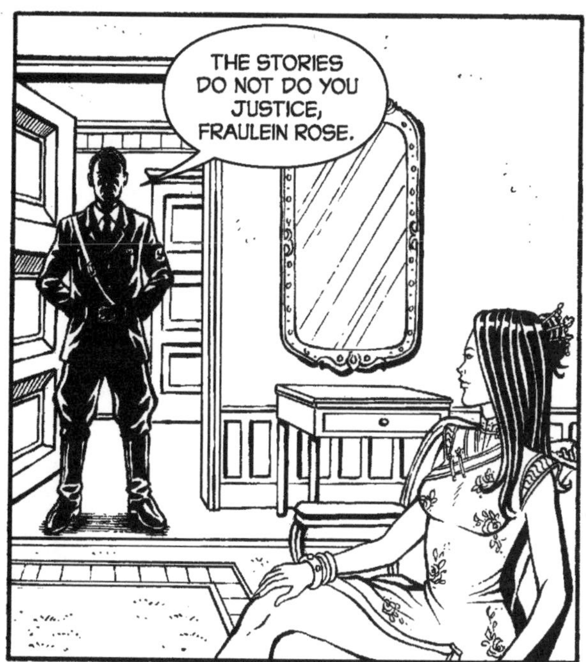
THE STORIES DO NOT DO YOU JUSTICE, FRAULEIN ROSE.

I COULD SAY THE SAME TO YOU, HERR HITLER. IT IS MY GREAT PLEASURE TO BRING YOU A MESSAGE FROM THOSE WHOSE LIVES YOU HAVE SO DEEPLY CHANGED...

BLAAAAM!
GO TO HELL.

WHAT—?

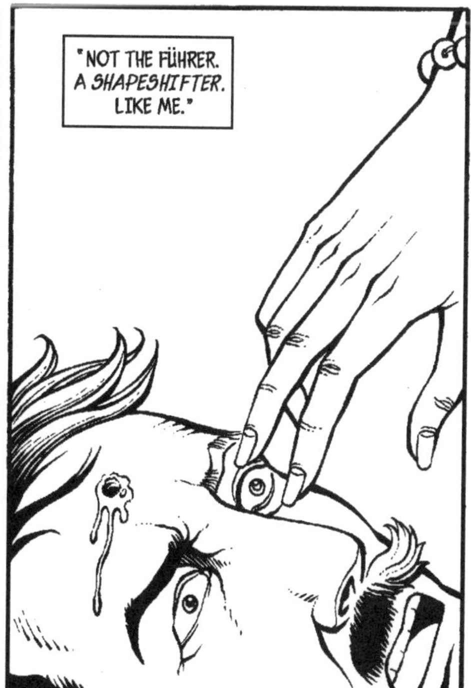
"NOT THE FÜHRER. A SHAPESHIFTER. LIKE ME."

THAT WILL BE QUITE ENOUGH, FRAULEIN ROSE. A SHAME THAT WE HAD TO LOSE ONE OF OUR MOST TALENTED DOPPELGANGERS, BUT HIS SACRIFICE WILL BE REMEMBERED.
SADLY, YOURS WILL NOT.
BOOOOSH!

GOEBBELS WAS RIGHT TO SUSPECT SOMETHING WAS AMISS WITH YOU, SWEETLING. A VILE MAN, BUT CLEVER.

YOU...AAAKKKKGH...CAN GO...TO HELL...TOO...
TELL ME HOW IT IS ONCE YOU ARRIVE, AND I'LL CONSIDER IT!

TAKE YOUR HANDS OFF HER.

YOU DARE TO THREATEN ME? WE ARE SURROUNDED BY THE FINEST OF THE REICH'S FORCES, BOTH MORTAL AND MÄCHTIG!
AND LEST YOU FORGET, DEAR CAPTAIN, I HAVE YOUR GIRLFRIEND'S THROAT IN MY FIST. THERE IS NOTHING YOU CAN DO TO ME FAST ENOUGH TO PREVENT ME FROM SNAPPING IT LIKE KINDLING.

CORRECTION: MY GIRLFRIEND, NOT HIS.
AND THERE IS SOMETHING I CAN DO...

"FELIPE CAN FORM HIS PORTALS ONLY WITHIN DENSELY PACKED MOLECULES--METAL, WOOD, STONE."
AHHHHHHHHHHHHHH!!!
"BUT WALLS DON'T FEEL ANYTHING WHEN THEIR MOLECULAR STRUCTURE IS DISRUPTED BY A TRANS-SPACE WARP."
"I GUESS YOU CAN'T SAY THE SAME FOR SUPERHUMAN FLESH."

SWOOOSH

AH...*MAHAL KO*, YOU'RE BLEEDING! RIGHT ABOVE YOUR *SCAR*.

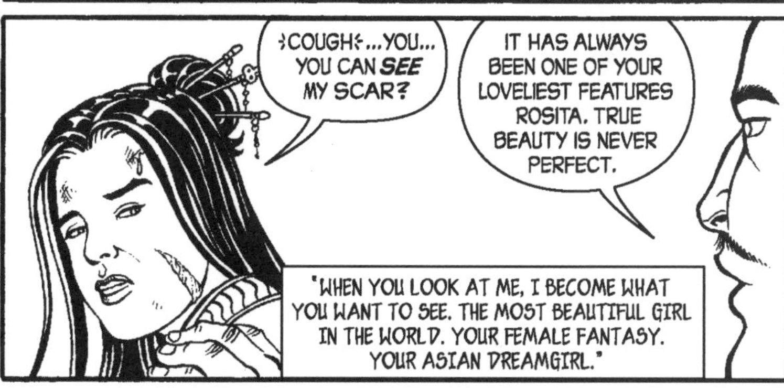
COUGH...YOU... YOU CAN *SEE* MY SCAR?
IT HAS ALWAYS BEEN ONE OF YOUR LOVELIEST FEATURES ROSITA. TRUE BEAUTY IS NEVER PERFECT.
"WHEN YOU LOOK AT ME, I BECOME WHAT YOU WANT TO SEE. THE MOST BEAUTIFUL GIRL IN THE WORLD. YOUR FEMALE FANTASY. YOUR ASIAN DREAMGIRL."

"AND IT TURNS OUT THAT FOR FELIPE... THAT WAS *ME* ALL ALONG."

"AFTER I GOT OUT OF THE HOSPITAL, I LET HIM TAKE ME OUT ON A *REAL* DATE. A MONTH LATER, I MARRIED HIM."

"OUR FIRST MISSION TOGETHER WAS OUR FINAL MISSION FOR XSF. THEY *NEVER* TOLD US WHAT PROJECT TERMINUS WAS--ONLY THAT BY EXTRACTING IT, WE HAD LIKELY ENDED THE WAR."

HIROSHIMA, JAPAN. 1945.
ENOLA GAY
"HISTORY IS A TRICKY THING. IN THE FOG OF WAR, YOU'RE JUST A SINGLE PIECE IN A PUZZLE THAT NO ONE TRULY UNDERSTANDS."
END

STORY: AMY CHU
PENCILS: LARRY HAMA • INKS: CRAIG YEUNG

START, DAMN YOU!
COUGH
SPUTTER

WE'VE KNOWN EACH OTHER FOR HOW LONG?
SINCE WE WERE... SIX? SEVEN?
YOU AND YOUR WHOLE FAMILY, ALWAYS LATE FOR EVERYTHING.

YEAH, I'LL TAKE THAT BUNCH. SHE'LL LOVE THOSE.

OH, MAKIKO— LOOK!

CRAP. TRAFFIC JAM!

HEY, WHAT'S GOING ON?
RECREATION CENTER

JACK, I DIDN'T THINK YOU WERE COMING. WE'RE JUST ABOUT TO CLOSE.
PUFF PUFF
GIVE
ARE YOU KIDDING? I CAN'T MISS A DATE WITH MY GIRL.

SURPRISE!!
OH...

HAPPY BIRTHDAY TO YOU
HAPPY BIRTHDAY TO YOU
SNIFF

I AM SOOO LATE...
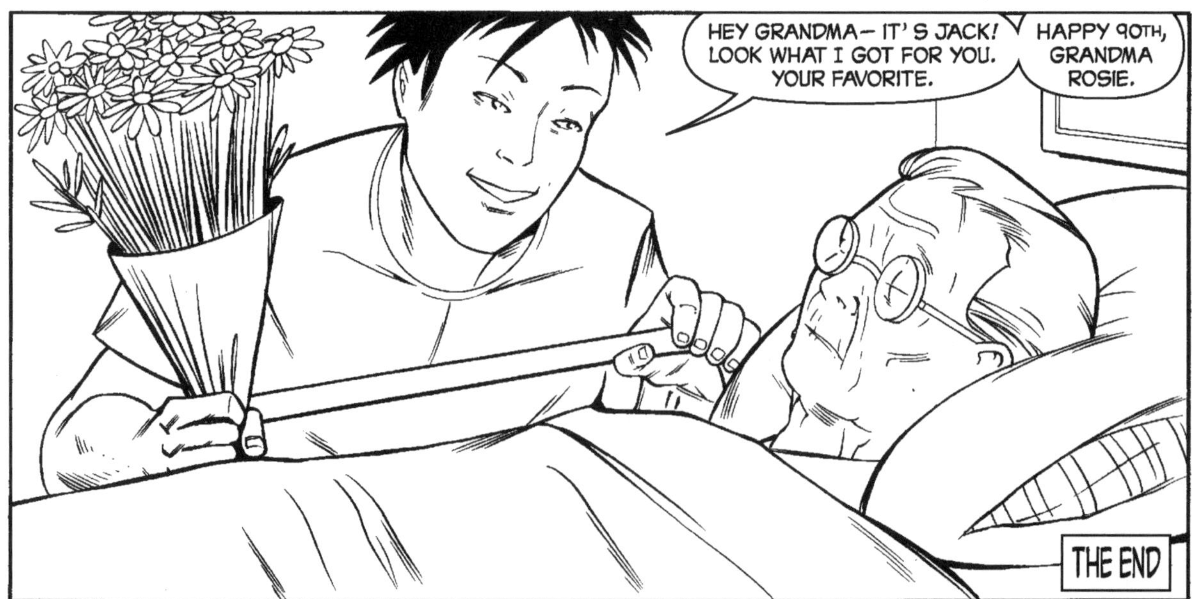
HEY GRANDMA– IT'S JACK! LOOK WHAT I GOT FOR YOU. YOUR FAVORITE.
HAPPY 90TH, GRANDMA ROSIE.
THE END

ADAM WARROCK

fan of comic books, video games, TV, nd movies, Adam dreamed of having uperpowers as a child, but grew up an rdinary adult with a boring job. After alling asleep at his desk one day, he wakes suddenly to find himself urrounded by the wreckage of what vas once his cubicle. The reason soon ecomes clear: When he raises his voice call for help, the resulting sonic vaves shatter the side of his building. ropelling himself through the hole and ut to freedom on pulsing ribbons of ound, he vows to use his powers to ollow his heart—and to help others do e same.

STORY: EUGENE AHN
ART: MING DOYLE

REVOLUTION SHUFFLE

STORY: BAO PHI
ART: GB TRAN

In the near future, a zombie outbreak sweeps across America, and fingers point to Asia as its source. Rampant suspicion and hostility prompts the authorities to round up and herd Asian Americans into "containment" camps, where they serve as human bait to lure the undead away from population centers. Far from other survivors, and surrounded by walking corpses, charismatic freedom fighter Lydia Tran, and her lieutenant, California Nguyen, set out to free the incarcerated—and lead an uprising against both the living and the dead.

TEMPEST

ike her namesake, Tempest is apricious, violent...and lethal. But the profession for which she's een trained, these characteristics re assets. Taken as a small child y The Fold, a covert organization f unknown origins, she has been ithlessly shaped into a merciless ller, gradually sacrificing different spects of her humanity in exchange or ever more deadly skills. On the ve of her 13th birthday, she has early become the perfect assassin: girl without memories, without ties others, without even a sense of elf. But she hasn't fully extinguished er ability to feel. After unknowingly urdering her twin during her graduation," Tempest sheds a tear nd escapes, vowing never to take nother life. Yet her battle has just egun: Hunted by The Fold, she ngs for peace, but the violent storm, ithin her and in the world around er, rages on.

STORY: KAI MA
ART: ERIC KIM

THE WALKMAN

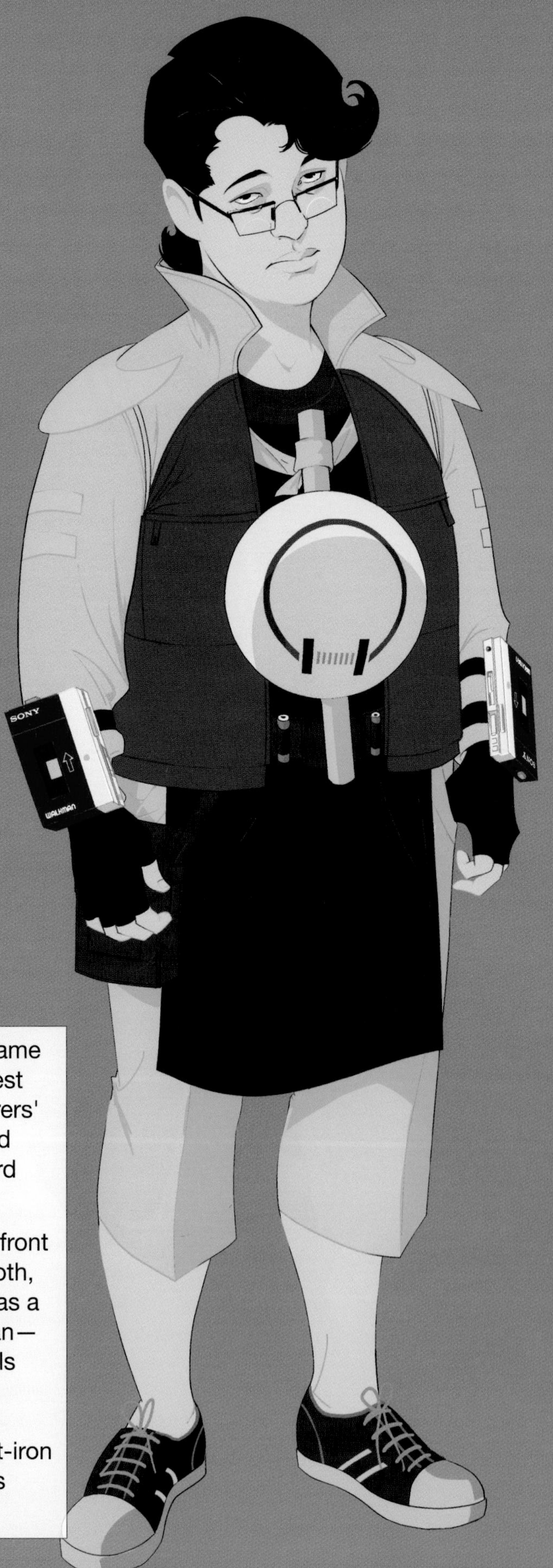

Anthony Le Pham rose to fame in the 80s as a child star best known for playing adventurers' sidekicks, gadget-obsessed geeks, and socially awkward exchange students.

After breaking up a fight in front of his empty autograph booth, he decides to battle crime as a vigilante called the Walkman—not "Wok-Man," as criminals frequently assume. Clad in armor made of jerry-rigged cassette players and a cast-iron wok, he special-delivers his own brand of justice.

STORY: AARON TAKAHASHI
ART: MUKESH SINGH

ANGRY ASIAN MAN

STORY: PHIL YU
ART: JERRY MA

aam---17-00003--epic
EARCHING.....
...SEARCHING.....
LOCATED....NY CITY
00136-8888-555-00059
1986---17-00003--star

Peter Min was just an average cubicle-dwelling drone. But when a freak power surge fuses his mind and body to the network, he finds himself wielding frightening new techno-conscious abilities: a lightning-fast, near-prescient capacity for comprehending data patterns and the explosive power to transmit electrical energy blasts at unsuspecting victims on the receiving end of a network connection. Now a living interface between man and machine, unable to block the constant surge of information through his brain, he must learn how to control his power...before it overcomes his humanity.

MEI THE ALIEN
STORY: KOJI STEVEN SAKAI
ART: DEODATA PANGANDOYON
Mei is an alien. Not the undocumented kind: She's literal from outer space. When she turned 10, her parents told her the shocking truth—that *all* Asians are secretly aliens It made sense to Mei, she reasoned. She was short, had almond-shaped eyes and was unnaturally good at math and science. Now, having discovered her own secret, she's determined to fulfill a new goal: Taking over the world...and then the universe!

side an internment camp in 1942, a
am of imprisoned Japanese Americans
ilds a robotic suit out of leftover metal
d wood. The armor is fixed with
eaponry that echoes the tradition of
murai, but reflects the reality around its
eators: It is equipped with stolen guns,
memade cannons and baseball bats.
e purpose of the suit is a mystery:
it meant to be worn, or is it simply an
borate protest-art project, conducted
while away the time? The answer
comes apparent when an unarmed
panese American dons it and begins
ing it to conduct clandestine missions
hasten the end of the war, and uplift
e spirits of those who have been
erned.

STORY: ERIC NAKAMURA
ART: SARA SAEDI

Uma Padwarthan is a detective with a unique background—she is a Dalit, a member of India's historically "untouchable" caste—and a special gift: She is a *sadhu*, or holy person, who is able to address troubles that her clients have with the dead. Reluctantly initiated into the Aghori way as an orphan, she is now weary of the dead and their games. She walks that path with resentment, practicing her art with loathing and a ferocious desire to be free. But in order to find peace and be released of her terrible burden, she must free no fewer than 111,111 souls.

STORY: THENMOZHI SOUNDARARAJAN
ART: SAUMIN SURESH PATEL

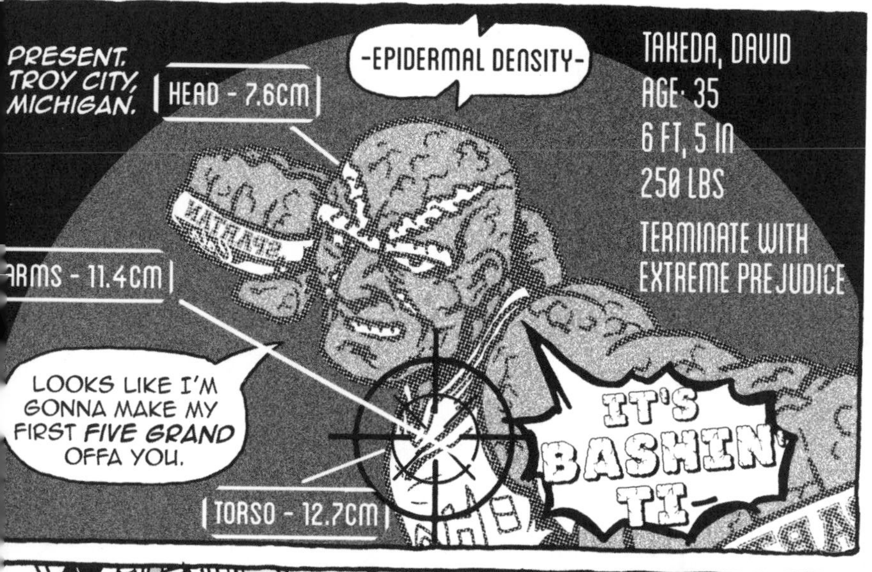
PRESENT. TROY CITY, MICHIGAN.
-EPIDERMAL DENSITY-
TAKEDA, DAVID
AGE: 35
6 FT, 5 IN
250 LBS
TERMINATE WITH EXTREME PREJUDICE
HEAD - 7.6CM
ARMS - 11.4CM
TORSO - 12.7CM
LOOKS LIKE I'M GONNA MAKE MY FIRST FIVE GRAND OFFA YOU.
IT'S BASHIN' TI

-STRATEGIC ATTACK POINT LOCATED-
UH-OH. NOT GOOD.
FACE - 3.1CM

THOOM!

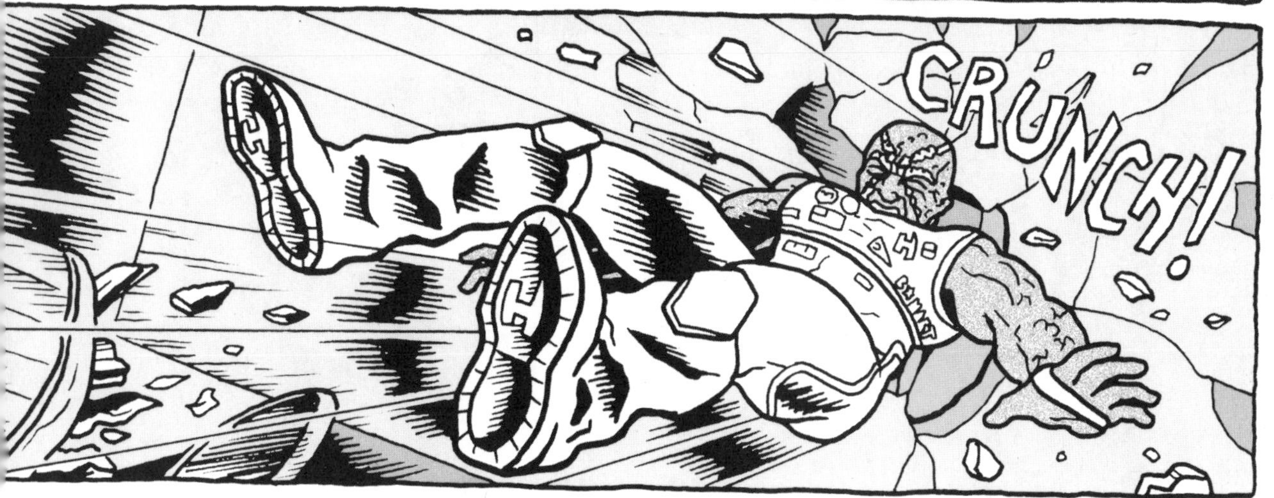
CRUNCH!

12 HOURS AGO

NEVADA, YUCCA FLATS—AREA 52

-ATOMIC PROGENY DIVISION-

IS BEING A WALKING BILLBOARD ANY WAY TO REPAY YOUR COUNTRY, DAVID? IS IT ANY WAY TO...HONOR THE DEAD?

SLAM!

I'M SURE THAT ONE DOESN'T COUNT.
SPARTAN Cola
NAW. STILL FELT PRETTY DAMN GOOD, THOUGH.

DAVID...I KNOW YOU BLAME ME FOR WHAT HAPPENED TO JEN. BUT DON'T PUNISH THE PEOPLE OF TROY FOR MY FAILURE. AND DON'T PUNISH THE PRESENT BECAUSE OF THE PAST.

SAVE THE INSPIRATIONAL CRAP, LOCKE. ME, I'M JUST LOOKIN' OUT FOR NUMBER--
WHEN'S THE LAST TIME YOU SAW THIS?

CLUNK

...1988.
KYOTO, JAPAN.
YA SURE THIS IS GONNA WORK, RAV?
INDUBITABLY. I CALIBRATED THE DETECTOR'S FREQUENCIES TO THE EXACT SPECIFICATIONS OF...

...THAT FRISBEE THING YOU SNAGGED FROM YOUR GRANDFATHER?
"RAVI'S GRANDDAD WAS SOME NUCLEAR RESEARCH BIGWIG. EVERY SUMMER, THEY RENTED THE HOUSE NEXT TO OURS WHEN HE CAME TO TOWN TO CONSULT WITH JAPAN'S ATOMIC ENERGY COMMISSION."

I TOLD YOU, DAVID--IT'S NOT A FRISBEE. ITS INTERNAL ARCHITECTURE SUGGESTS A DYNAMIC CONTAINMENT UNIT FOR SOME KIND OF MATERIALLY ALTERED HEAVY ELEMENT.
MY GRANDPAPA SAYS THEY FOUND THESE BURIED IN KEY LOCATIONS THROUGHOUT HIROSHIMA AND NAGASAKI--EMPTY, OF COURSE, LIKE THIS ONE, BUT BLAH BLAH BLAH, BIG-WORD FORMULA...

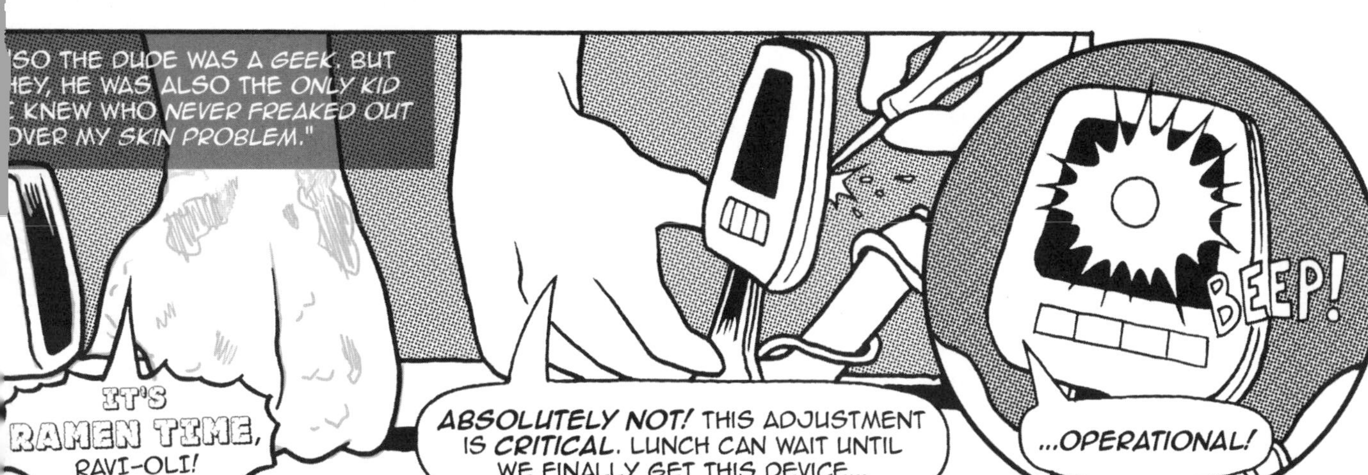
"SO THE DUDE WAS A GEEK. BUT HEY, HE WAS ALSO THE ONLY KID I KNEW WHO NEVER FREAKED OUT OVER MY SKIN PROBLEM."
IT'S RAMEN TIME, RAVI-OLI!
ABSOLUTELY NOT! THIS ADJUSTMENT IS CRITICAL. LUNCH CAN WAIT UNTIL WE FINALLY GET THIS DEVICE...
BEEP!
...OPERATIONAL!

OH, YEAH! OH, YEAH! TEAM HIDE AND SIKH ARE IN THE HOUSE...

YEAH, OK, WE GOTTA GET A BETTER NAME.
SO, UH, WHADDAYA GONNA DO WITH THIS THING AGAIN?

HAVE YOU NOT BEEN LISTENING TO A WORD I'VE SAID ALL SUMMER? FAT MAN AND LITTLE BOY.
UH...I KINDA LIKE "HIDE AND SIKH" BETTER...

I MEAN THE NUCLEAR BOMBS! HIROSHIMA AND NAGASAKI WERE THE TWO CITIES TARGETED BY THE AMERICAN MILITARY FOR ATOMIC ATTACK DURING THE WAR. YOU SHOULD KNOW THIS: YOUR GRANDFATHER WAS A SURVIVOR.

BUT THEY WEREN'T THE ONLY ONES. HIS CITY, WHERE WE ARE RIGHT NOW, WAS ALSO ON THE LIST. IT WAS REMOVED AT THE LAST MINUTE BECAUSE THE U.S. SECRETARY OF STATE HAD HONEYMOONED HERE.

SO, LOGIC DICTATES THERE SHOULD BE PODS LIKE THIS ONE BURIED HERE AS WELL--EXCEPT THEY WON'T BE EMPTY.

AND TOMORROW WE'LL USE THIS **DETECTOR** AND *FIND THEM*.
YOU'LL *USE IT*. JUST LIKE YOU'VE BEEN USING THIS ***LUNK***.
I'LL USE IT. JUST LIKE I'VE BEEN USING YOU, *YOU* **LUNK**.

WHAT'D YOU SAY, RAV?
I...AH...NOTHING. I BELIEVE I'M SUFFERING FROM *LOW BLOOD SUGAR*, DAVID. LET'S GO GET THOSE **NOODLES**
OH YEAH, IT'S RAMEN TIME!
...MUST YOU **ALWAY** SHOUT THAT?

THE NEXT MORNING.
RIGHT HERE, ***DAVID!***
THIS IS, LIKE, OUR ***SEVENTH HOLE***. IF THIS ONE'S A ***BUST*** TOO, CAN WE CALL IT A DAY?
I'VE ADJUSTED THE *SENSOR PARAMETERS*, AND I FEEL CERTAIN THIS IS ***A CACHE***.
SO PLEASE--DIG *CAREFULLY*. THE PODS MAY BE ***UNSTABLE*** AFTER SO MANY YEARS.

I FIGURE THE *FASTER* I DIG, THE *FASTER* WE CAN GO HOM
DAVID, REALLY...

HEY, WE FOUND ONE!

UH, RAV, SHOULD THIS BE ***HAPPENING?***
YOU ***IDIOT***. WHA HAVE YOU DONE-
VREE
VREE
VREE

AAAAARRRRGGHHHH!
FSST
FSST

THE PODS!

COUGH
COUGH
I JUST GOT EXPLODED AND YOU'RE WORRYING ABOUT YOUR STUPID PODS?

SNAP!
HOLY...WHAT'S GOING ON?

I'M, LIKE, TWO FEET TALLER THAN YOU NOW!

THOSE WERE **MY PODS**, YOU DUMB OX!

RAVI, I *DIDN'T* MEAN TO...
YOU... YOU...
STOLE THEM!

"OVER THE NEXT FEW WEEKS, MY BODY STARTED *CHANGING*. MY PARENTS SENT ME TO DOCTORS, SCIENTISTS--*NONE OF 'EM* COULD EXPLAIN WHAT WAS HAPPENING. I KNEW THERE WAS ONLY *ONE GUY* WHO COULD."
RAVI, ***PLEASE***-- OPEN THE DOOR!

I DON'T KNOW WHAT'S HAPPENING TO ME!
THERE MUST BE ***OTHERS***. *THERE MUST BE*. WE'LL FIND THEM...WE'LL FIND THEM ***ALL***.
Sea of Japan
HONSHU
Tohoku
Kansai
SHIKOKU
KYUSHU

AND THAT WAS THE LAST TIME I EVER SAW HIM. WHERE'D YOU GET THIS, ANYWAY?
WE FOUND IT AMONG THE OTHERS AT HIS GRANDFATHER'S LAST KNOWN LOCATION.
TIK

WERE THOSE ALL...EMPTY?

YES. AND THAT, DAVID, IS WHY WE NEED YOUR HELP.
"DAVID..."

OUR GAME OF-- WHAT DID YOU CALL IT? "HIDE AND SIKH"?-- HAS GROWN TIRESOME.

SO COME OUT, COME OUT, WHEREVER YOU ARE...

NOT THAT I RELISH SEEING WHAT YOU'VE BECOME AGAIN. YOU WERE UGLY BEFORE YOUR UNCONTROLLED EXPOSURE TO THE VARIABLY REACTIVE ISOTOPIC LUCIFERIUM, BUT NOW...DO YOU REALLY KISS YOUR MOTHER WITH THAT FACE?

NO, BUT I KISSED YOURS THE OTHER NIGHT.

AH, I SEE THE EFFECTS OF RANDOM MUTATION HAVEN'T BLUNTED YOUR CRUDE WIT.

THE ACHE IN MY JAW SAYS YOU'VE POWERED UP TOO, RAV. SO WHY D'YOU LOOK NORMAL? WHY DIDN'T THE... VOLLEYBALL RENUCTIVE...
DON'T HURT YOURSELF, DAVID. VRIL. CALL IT VRIL.
VRIL IS A CRYSTALLINE VARIANT OF GOLD, CAPABLE OF STORING AND TRANSLATING ENERGY. LIKE GOLD, IT CAN BOND WITH LIVING DNA-- THOUGH IN YOUR CASE, IT SEEMS TO HAVE EXAGGERATED MUTATIONS YOU INHERITED FROM YOUR RADIATION-EXPOSED GRANDFATHER.

AND LIKE GOLD, IT CAN BE READILY INCORPORATED INTO TECHNOLOGY, USIN A NANOPARTICLE MATRIX TO ACTUATE CHANGE AT THE ATOMIC LEVEL--
BLAH BLAH BLAH, BIG-WORD FORMU I GET IT. I JUST HIT MY DAILY SCIENTIFIC MUMBO JUMBO QUOT

AND YOU KNOW WHAT? NOW I FEEL LIKE HITTIN' SOMETHIN' ELSE. LIKE MAYBE TEN GRAND WORTH OF SOMETHIN' ELSE.

IT'S BASHIN' TIME!
CHA--

--CHING?
PANG!
CHAK
CHAK
CHAK
I'M GLAD YOU'VE DISCOVERED A NEW CATCHPHRASE. AS YOU WISH, OLD FRIEND.
COMPUTER--SET BATTLE MODE TO "BASHING TIME."
-STRATEGIC ATTACK POINT LOCATED-
NEXT CHAPTE "THE ALIE PERIL: WELCO TO THE TERR
CHAK
CHAK
CHAK
AW, MAN...HERE WE GO AGAIN...

THE POWER OF PETUNIA

STORY: JOY OSMANSKI
ART: YASMIN LIANG

WHY DIDN'T YOU MAKE HIM WEAR HIS HELMET? USELESS! IF YOU WERE ANY KIND OF A MOTHER, THIS WOULD HAVE NEVER HAPPENED!
IT'S YOUR FAULT HE'S GONE!
MY FAULT? YOU WEREN'T HERE...YOU'RE NEVER HERE! YOU CARE MORE ABOUT YOUR STUPID GRAD STUDENTS THAN YOUR OWN CHILDREN!
IF YOU EVER PAID ANY ATTENTION TO HIM, HE'D STILL BE HERE...
HE'D STILL BE HERE!
SIX MONTHS LATER...
PETUNIA!
I HAVE A SEMINAR. I'LL BE OUT LATE. I PICKED UP DINNER--IT'S ON THE TABLE. BE SURE YOU CLEAR UP AFTER AND DO YOUR HOMEWORK.
CROSSWORD PUZZLES
WHAT'S SHE GONNA DO, STAY IN THERE FOREVER? NOT THAT I CARE.
BED BY EIGHT, PETUNIA.

WHAT ARE YOU DOING?
TRYING TO GET OUT.
CAN I HELP YOU?
NO. NO ONE CAN HELP ME.
WHY NOT?
BECAUSE NO ONE KNOWS THE SECRET PASSWORD.
---IS THIS IT?
WHO ARE YOU? HOW DID YOU KNOW--
CROSSWORD PUZZLES

PETUNA DREAMS AGAIN...
WHAT ARE YOU DOING HERE ALONE?
I WENT AWAY, AND NO ONE MISSES ME.
CAN I HELP YOU?
NO. NO ONE CAN HELP ME.
WHY NOT?
BECAUSE AFRAID YO LEAVE ME NEED TO K YOU'LL NE LEAVE M
DAD?
f o r g i
THE BEGI

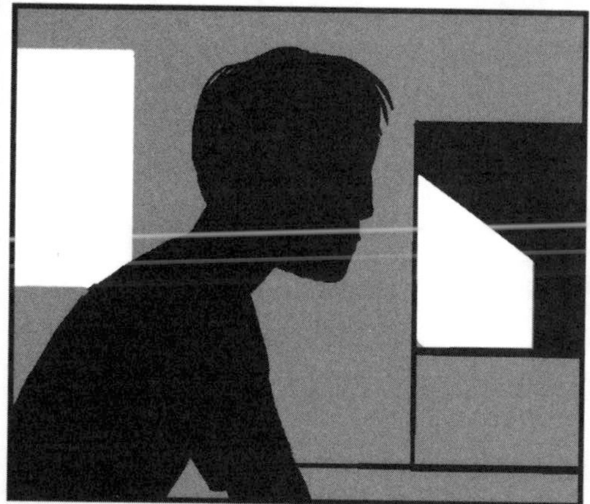

STORY: PAUL WEI
ART: CHI-YUN LAU

TED, WE WEREN'T SURE YOU WERE QUALIFIED WHEN WE PROMOTED YOU, BUT YOU'VE REALLY FIT RIGHT IN.

WELL, YOU PICKED THE RIGHT MAN FOR THE JOB, SIR.

MING'S A BRILLIANT GUY, BUT HE'S GOT THE PEOPLE SKILLS OF A ROBOT.

SOMEONE LIKE ME, I KNOW HOW TO GET THE WORKER BEES TO RESPOND.

TIK

NOW WATCH THIS DRIVE.

BOOM!!

THE NEXT DAY.

WELL, TED COULDN'T MANAGE HIS WAY OUT OF A MONOMOLECULAR MEMBRANE!

WHO WOULD'VE THOUGHT GOLF COULD BE SO DEADLY? AT LEAST FOR TED...

GLAD TO HAVE YOU IN CHARGE NOW, KEN.

ONE WEEK LATER.

THIS IS A SWEATSHOP! A WELL-LIT, AIR-CONDITIONED SWEATSHOP!

AND I CAN'T WORK BEYOND MY CONTRACTUAL 40 HOU PER WEEK. I HAVE A SPOUSAL UNIT AND OFFSPRING.

MY JOB DESCRIPTION DOESN'T INCLUDE THERMAL DYNAMICS.

YOU'D BETTER DO SOMETHING ABOUT ALL OF THIS, MING. OR GET USED TO DOING THINGS ALL BY YOURSELF!

WELL DONE, KEN! YOUR NEW ROBOCENTRIC BUSINESS MODEL HAS TURN THIS INTO THE COMPANY'S MOST LUCRATIVE DEPARTMENT. WE SHOULD STA REPLACING THE COMPANY'S REMAINING NON-VALUE-ADDING MEMBERS AS

ONE MONTH LATER.

CAMDEN'S REVENGE

SHATTERED

BAKE SALE! TUES.

OOH, SEVEN--A NEW RECORD! NICE JOB, BABE.

STORY: KEIKO AGENA
ART: LOUIE CHIN

IT'S ALREADY UP ON YOUTUBE. "BOBA NOSE WONG GETS A BATH" IS PROBABLY GONNA BEAT OUT "TRASHCAN WONG ROLLS DOWNHILL."
I'M SO SORRY, MARK...

IT'S OKAY, CAMDEN. IT'S JUST--THE RULES. THE POPULAR KIDS DUMP ON THE LOSERS.
I'M JUST GLAD AT LEAST ONE OF US FIGURED OUT HOW TO BE POPULAR.

Math IS EASY

NOW WE'LL SEE WHO THE REAL LOSER IS, ANNALIE.

OW COULD WE BE FRIENDS WITH YOU, JULIE? YOU JUST OULDN'T FIT IN. AND THAT I MEAN YOU OULDN'T FIT IN MY CAR, WIDE-LOAD JULIE RHODES!
GOOD ONE, ANNALIE!
LUNCHTIME, GIRLS-- DELICIOUS NO-CAL KALE SMOOTHIES!

UGH. CAMDEN, WHAT SEWER DID YOU GET THIS STUFF FROM?
YOU KNOW WHAT THEY SAY--THE WORSE IT TASTES, THE BETTER IT IS FOR YOU.

WHY ARE YOU SO HAPPY?
YOU'LL SEE.

CAN YOU BELIEVE IT?!
WHAT WERE THEY THINKING?

WHOA! PRETTY BADASS, ANNALIE.
YOU GUYS ROCK.
I'M TOTALLY SHAVING MY HEAD TONIGHT.
WHAT ARE YOU GUYS TALKING ABOUT?
ARE YOU ALL JUST A BUNCH OF SHEEP? THEY LOOK RIDICULOUS!
HAVING HAIR IS 24 HOU AGO.
CAMDEN HIGA, JUST BECAUSE YOU'RE OFF TREND DOESN'T MEAN YOU HAVE TO BE JEALOUS.
CAMDEN? MORE LIKE CAM-DONE. YOU'RE A LOSER. AND YOU... ARE... OUT!
THOSE HATEFUL LITTLE...
I WAS TOO EASY ON THEM. TOO MERCIFUL.
BEING BALD JUST ISN'T PERMANENT ENOUGH FOR THOSE BI--
MARK?

SORRY, CAM. YOUR MOM LET ME IN.

SO... YOU KNOW.

WELL, THEN *HELP* ME! NO ONE'S BETTER AT ORGANIC CHEMISTRY THAN YOU ARE. WE COULD GIVE THEM PERMANENTLY CROSSED EYES.

TURN THEM BLUE. WE COULD MAKE THEM *FAT*...

LET IT GO, CAM.

LET IT GO? YOU SHOULD BE THANKING ME! THE WAY THOSE GUYS TREAT YOU...

THEY ONLY HAVE POWER BECAUSE YOU AND EVERYONE ELSE GIVES THEM POWER.

BECAUSE YOU CARE WHAT THEY THINK.

BECAUSE YOU PLAY BY THEIR RULES.

WELL, IF IT ISN'T MR. AND MRS. LOSER...

DID YOU HEAR SOMETHING... MRS. LOSER?
CAN'T SAY I DID... MR. LOSER.

WHOA.

METATRON

STORY & ART: STUART NG

FLEETS 3 TO 7 CONFIRMED KIA, ALL HANDS LOST. FLEET 2 MIA--NO COMMUNICATION.

REMAINING FORCES ORDERED TO DEPLOY TO THE FRONT **IMMEDIATELY**.

ENEMY INCOMING ETA 1 MINUTE. PILOTS ORDERED TO CONVERGE AT CQC RANGE AND ENGAGE. FORMATION OMEGA. AND...GODSPEED.

ROGER, SIR.

ALL WINGS: FORM UP. THIS IS WHERE WE MAKE OUR STAND. NO BACK UP. NO REINFORCEMENTS. NO QUARTER. WE DRAW THE LINE HERE. THIS IS WHERE WE WIN OR LOSE.

TIME TO MAKE 'EM PA

CHOOSE TO WIN!

THIS IS LUNAR BASE. METATRON, COME IN IMMEDIATELY!

DAMN IT!

*SECOND FLEET INCOMING, DELTA SECTOR! WE HA-- *BZZT**

THE DOCTOR SAYS SHE DOESN'T HAVE LONG.

SHE'LL LIVE. SHE JUST HAS TO MAKE THE CHOICE.

WE ALL CHOOSE TO LIVE OR DIE...
MOM...THE SKY...
JOY! THANK GOD. WE'RE STILL TRYING TO FIGURE OUT WHAT HAPPENED. ONE MOMENT LUNAR BASE WAS UNDER ATTACK, AND THE NEXT--THE ENEMY WAS...GONE.
MOM, WHERE'S DAD?
HONEY...YOUR FATHER DID A VERY BRAVE THING...
EN

LOS ROBOS, ARIZONA

SKY CORPS ACADEMY. LOS ROBOS, ARIZONA.

WE DON'T KNOW WHERE THEY'RE FROM OR WHY THEY COME.

BUT SIXTY YEARS AGO TODAY, THE FIRST RECORDED *TITAN ROBO* FROM OUTER SPACE DESCENDED UPON AN ARIZONA MOUNTAIN RANGE...

...AND BEFRIENDED A BOY SCOUT NAMED *SKIP TANAKA.*

TOGETHER, SKIP AND HIS TITAN ROBO BUDDY DEFENDED THE NATION FROM CRISIS AFTER CRISIS, SAVING LIVES, WINNING HEARTS, AND INSPIRING GENERATIONS.

TODAY, WE OF THE *SKY CORPS* CARRY ON CAPTAIN TANAKA'S LEGACY, TRAINING THE NATION'S BEST AND BRIGHTEST YOUTHS TO BE THE GREATEST PILOTS, CITIZENS, AND LEADERS THE WORLD HAS EVER SEEN.
BECAUSE EVERY FOUR YEARS, ANOTHER GROUP OF GIANT ROBOTS ARRIVES TO BOND WITH A BRAND NEW CROP OF CADETS.
AND SOME DAY, ONE OF THOSE CADETS MIGHT BE *YOU.*
STANFORD!

STORY: GREG PAK
ART: TAKESHI MIYAZAWA

<WAKE UP!>*
<WE'RE **WORKING** HERE.>
OKAY, OKAY.
<DON'T OKAY ME.>
MA...
*TRANSLATED FROM CHINESE

YOU KNOW, IF YOU'RE GOING TO **DISRUPT** THE **CEREMONY,** YOU MIGHT HAVE THE COURTESY TO DO IT IN **ENGLISH.**
BUT NOW, LET'S HEAR IT FOR TODAY'S CHOSEN CADETS!
SANCHEZ! OLIVETTI! PARK!
FRONT AND CENTER!

HEY!

GO ON. CLEAN IT UP.
THAT'S WHAT YOU'RE HERE FOR, ISN'T IT?

<STANFORD! CALM DOWN!>
BUT HE CAN'T--HE CAN'T--
<**WRONG...**>

"<...HE CAN DO WHATEVER HE WANTS.>"

THREE HOURS LATER...
HEY! HERE THEY COME!

VOOP.
VEEP.
HOOOLEEE COW.

VOOP.
VEEP.
HI.
Omigod omigod omigod.

WHERE'S...
...WHERE'S *MY* ROBO?
DON'T WORRY, SON.
I'M ON IT.
PARK
PARK
PARK

THREE MILES AWAY
Tch.
CLEAN IT UP.
IT'S WHAT YOU'RE HERE FOR, HUH?
?
VEEEE?
HOOO BOY.

VEEEE.
Um...

...I THINK THIS IS YOURS.

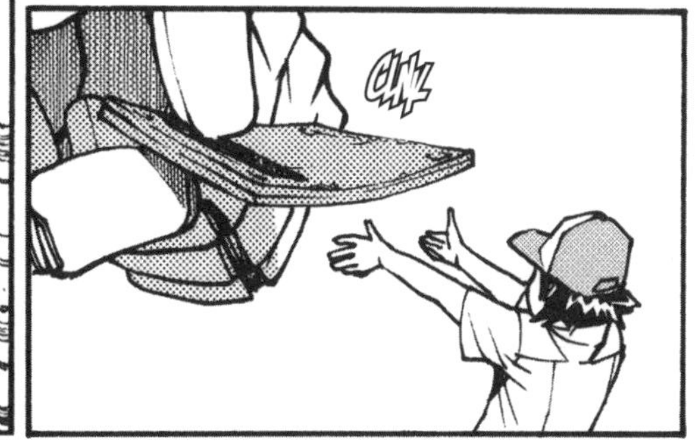
CLNK

CLNK
HA!
SO...THE MOUNTAIN'S OVER THERE.

SKY CORP
YOU'RE PRETTY LATE. YOU SHOULD PROBABLY--
KRRK

SKY CORP

HA.
HAOOEEEE!
YOUR ATTENTION, PLEASE!

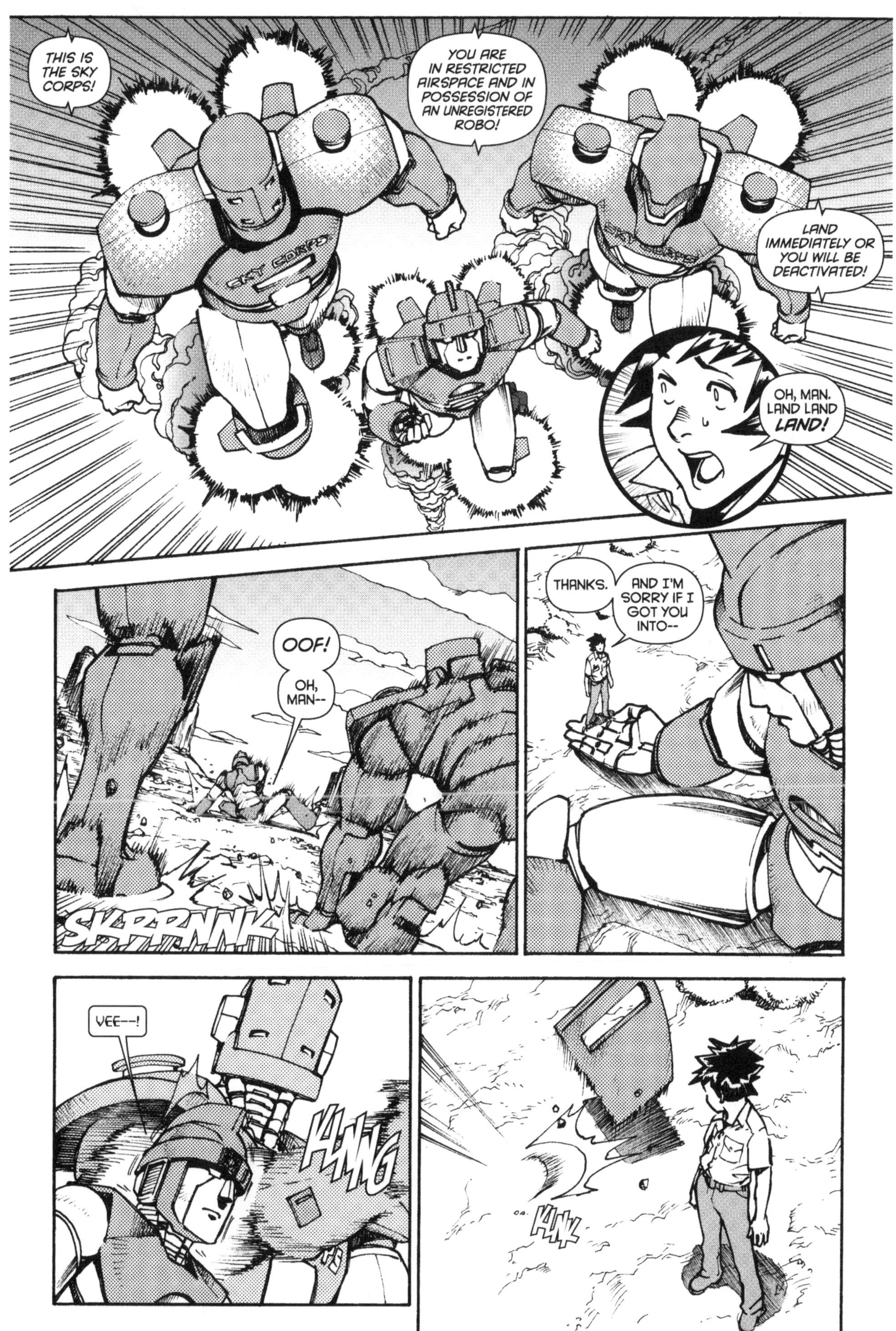
THIS IS THE SKY CORPS!
YOU ARE IN RESTRICTED AIRSPACE AND IN POSSESSION OF AN UNREGISTERED ROBO!
LAND IMMEDIATELY OR YOU WILL BE DEACTIVATED!
OH, MAN. LAND LAND LAND!
OOF!
OH, MAN--
SKRRNNK
THANKS.
AND I'M SORRY IF I GOT YOU INTO--
VEE--!
KLANG
KLUNK

HERE YOU GO.

HEY!

VEEE!
NO! LEAVE HIM ALONE!
STAND DOWN OR YOU WILL BE DEACTIVATED!

DANG IT ALL. THIS ISN'T RIGHT.
THE GENERAL'S ORDERS WERE VERY SPECIFIC, SIR. WE CAN'T--
"CAN'T"? DON'T HAVE MUCH USE FOR THAT WORD, SON.

NOW HOW 'BOUT LET'S RETHINK THIS.
C-CAPTAIN TANAKA?

LATER
<WELL. YOU LOOK NICE.>
THANKS, MA.
ALL RIGHT, CADETS!
WELCOME TO THE SKY!
LOS ROBOS, ARIZONA
written by GREG PAK art by TAKESHI MIYAZAWA lettering by SIMON BOWLAND

MEANWHILE
"I KNOW YOU'RE ANGRY."

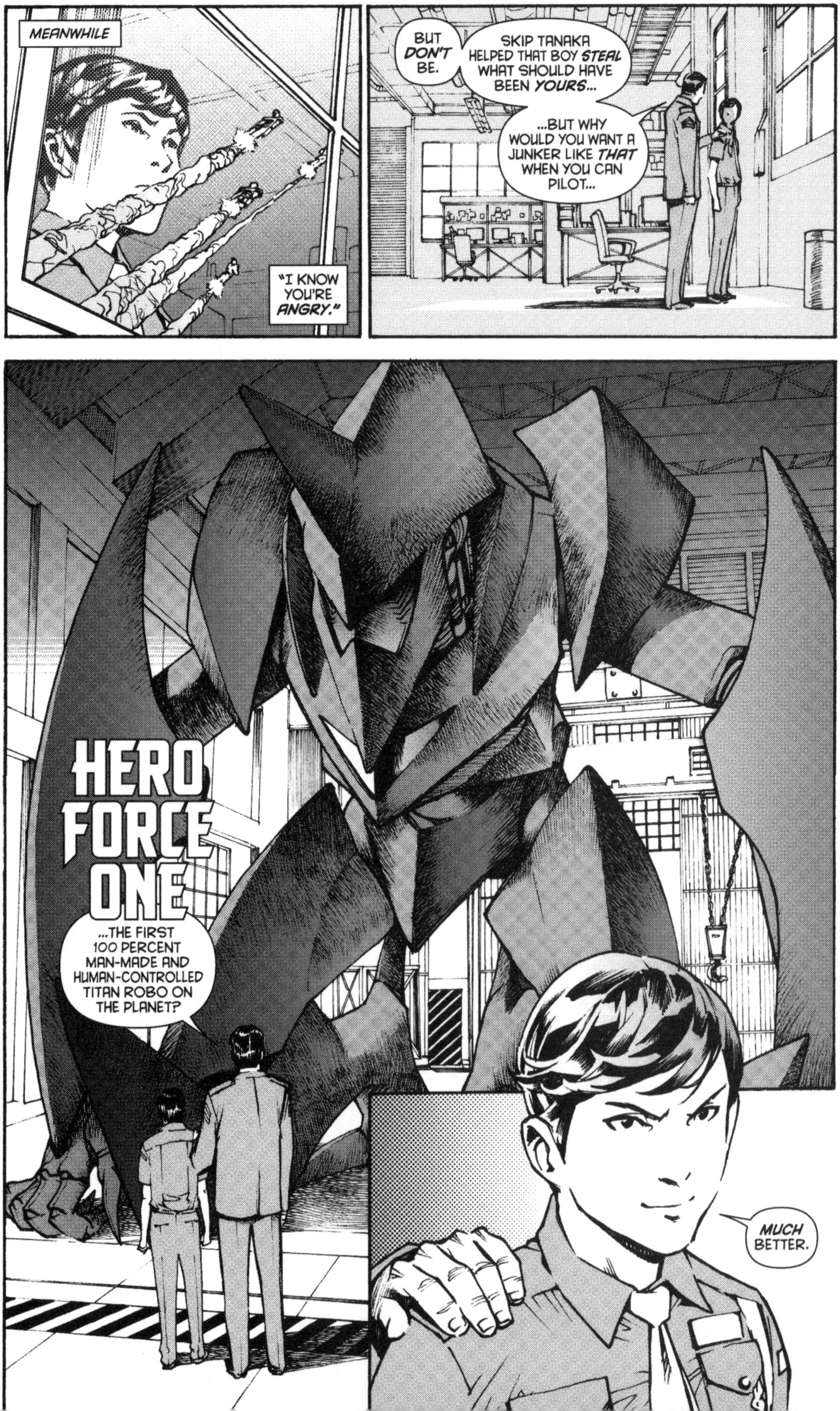

BUT DON'T BE.
SKIP TANAKA HELPED THAT BOY STEAL WHAT SHOULD HAVE BEEN YOURS...
...BUT WHY WOULD YOU WANT A JUNKER LIKE THAT WHEN YOU CAN PILOT...

HERO FORCE ONE

...THE FIRST 100 PERCENT MAN-MADE AND HUMAN-CONTROLLED TITAN ROBO ON THE PLANET?

MUCH BETTER.

JOLTING TALES OF STUDENTS
FROM THE FEARSOME FAR EAST
THAT WE DARE
YOU TO READ!

EYES

BRAIN

LIVE

HEART

ANATOMY

IN THIS ISSUE:
A PUPIL PROVES HE IS
A CUT ABOVE THE REST!

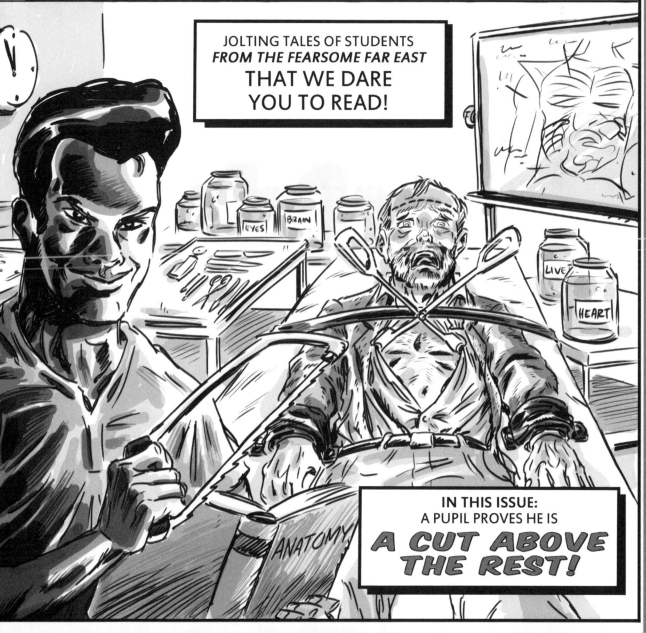

STORY: JAMIE FORD
ART: A.L. BAROZA

A SHARP SCALPEL MEANS AN EASY ***AAAAAAAAAAAAAAAIIIIIIEEEEE!!***

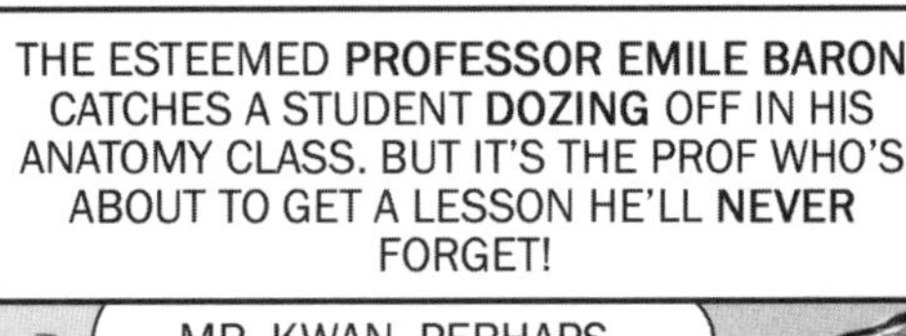
THE ESTEEMED PROFESSOR EMILE BARON CATCHES A STUDENT DOZING OFF IN HIS ANATOMY CLASS. BUT IT'S THE PROF WHO'S ABOUT TO GET A LESSON HE'LL NEVER FORGET!

MR. KWAN, PERHAPS YOU CAN SHARE WITH US THE MAJOR STRUCTURES OF THE BRAIN?
HUH? WHA?
YOU'VE BEEN NODDING OFF IN CLASS FOR WEEKS, AND I'VE HAD ENOUGH.

YOU ORIENTALS ARE SUPPOSED TO BE GOOD AT SCIENCE! UNLESS YOU GET A PERFECT SCORE ON THE EXAM TOMORROW, I'M GOING TO FAIL YOU...ON PRINCIPLE!
BUT IF I FAIL THIS CLASS, I'LL LOSE MY SCHOLARSHIP...AND I'VE BEEN WORKING EXTRA SHIFTS TO SUPPORT MY FAMILY.
HOW DO YOU EXPECT ME TO GET A PERFECT SCORE?

USE THIS, MR. KWAN.
JUST USE THIS!

MMMMFFFFZZZZZZZZ.
AUDITORIUM

WHAT HAPPENED?
WHERE AM I?

HELLO, PROFESSOR. I DECIDED TO FOLLOW YOUR ADVICE.
NOW...LET'S BEGIN OUR REVIEW OF THE MAJOR STRUCTURES OF THE BRAIN...

AAAAAHH!

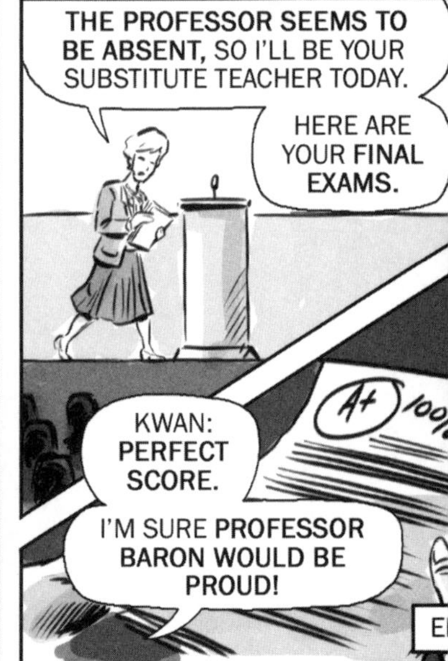
THE PROFESSOR SEEMS TO BE ABSENT, SO I'LL BE YOUR SUBSTITUTE TEACHER TODAY.
HERE ARE YOUR FINAL EXAMS.
A+
KWAN: PERFECT SCORE.
I'M SURE PROFESSOR BARON WOULD BE PROUD!

STORY: KEITH CHOW
ART: JEF CASTRO

GOLDFIELD, ARIZONA. 1900.
TOWER & WHITE MINING CO.

EVENING, EBENS.
MIKE.

HYUUUUU

CRK

‹GET AWAY FROM AH WONG, YOU DEVILS!›

CLICK

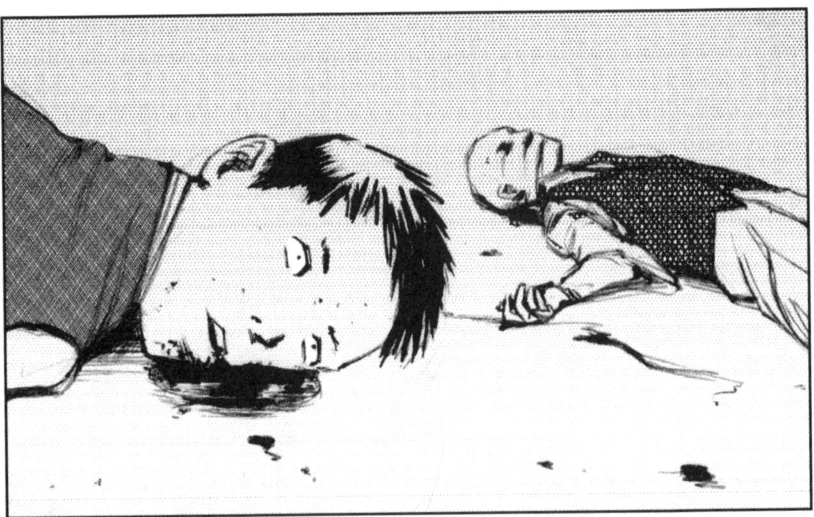

PERIL: WELCOME TO THE TERROR

PHOENIX, ARIZONA. PRESENT DAY. PHOENICIAN UNIVERSITY*
MASON WONG, SON OF IMPRISONED BIOPHYSICIST DR. BENJAMIN WONG KIN-LUN, HAS SPENT THE LAST MONTH ON A CROSS-COUNTRY HUNT FOR NANOTECH-POWERED PROTOTYPES CO-DEVELOPED BY HIS FATHER AND HIS FATHER'S RESEARCH PARTNER, DR. MALCOLM EADY. THAT SEARCH HAS NOW BROUGHT HIM BACK FULL CIRCLE--TO HIS COLLEGE ALMA MATER.
AN UNIVERSITY
SB1177
*NOW A DIVISION OF TOWER EDUCATIONAL SYSTEMS, INC.

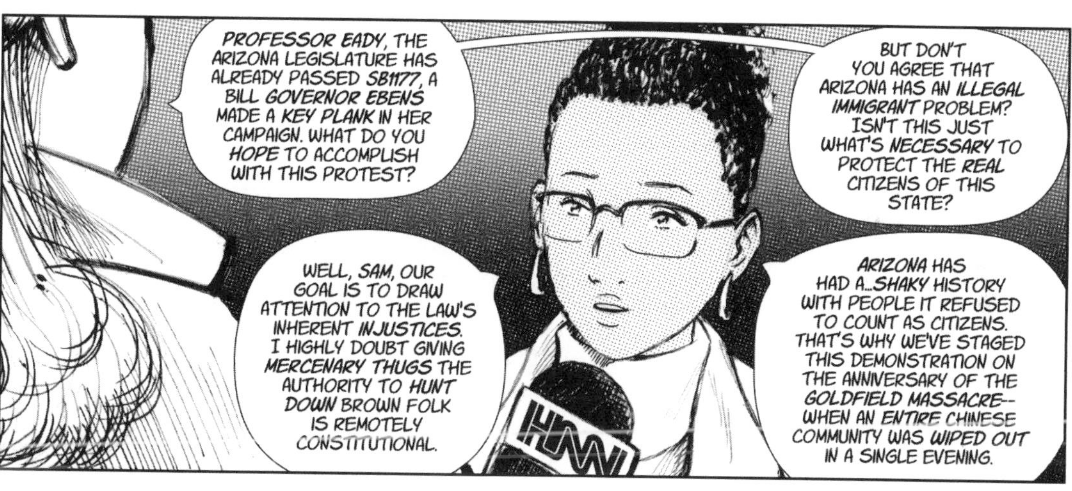
PROFESSOR EADY, THE ARIZONA LEGISLATURE HAS ALREADY PASSED SB1177, A BILL GOVERNOR EBENS MADE A KEY PLANK IN HER CAMPAIGN. WHAT DO YOU HOPE TO ACCOMPLISH WITH THIS PROTEST?
WELL, SAM, OUR GOAL IS TO DRAW ATTENTION TO THE LAW'S INHERENT INJUSTICES. I HIGHLY DOUBT GIVING MERCENARY THUGS THE AUTHORITY TO HUNT DOWN BROWN FOLK IS REMOTELY CONSTITUTIONAL.
BUT DON'T YOU AGREE THAT ARIZONA HAS AN ILLEGAL IMMIGRANT PROBLEM? ISN'T THIS JUST WHAT'S NECESSARY TO PROTECT THE REAL CITIZENS OF THIS STATE?
ARIZONA HAS HAD A...SHAKY HISTORY WITH PEOPLE IT REFUSED TO COUNT AS CITIZENS. THAT'S WHY WE'VE STAGED THIS DEMONSTRATION ON THE ANNIVERSARY OF THE GOLDFIELD MASSACRE-- WHEN AN ENTIRE CHINESE COMMUNITY WAS WIPED OUT IN A SINGLE EVENING.

PROFESSOR EADY, CAN WE HAVE A WORD WITH YOU?

HOW MAY I HELP YOU GENTLEMEN?
WE HAVE REASON TO BELIEVE YOU'VE BEEN IN CONTACT WITH THIS MAN: MASON WONG.

MASON? WE HAVEN'T SEEN EACH OTHER SINCE WE WERE KIDS.
IS THAT RIGHT?

SECURITY CAMERA 5-14

SECURITY CAMERA 5-17
SO I ASSUME YOU ALSO DON'T KNOW ANYTHING ABOUT THE BREAK-IN AT THE TOWER FACILITY IN FLAGSTAFF LAST NIGHT?

IF I'M NOT MISTAKEN, ISN'T THAT YOUR FIANCÉ, ZUHAIR MALIK?

RIGHT NOW, YOUR BOYFRIEND IS IN CUSTODY FOR AIDING AND ABETTING A TERRORIST.

UNLESS YOU HELP US, THEY'LL TURN HIM OVER TO THE FBI, THE CIA...OR WORSE: US.
AND WHAT IF I DON'T HELP YOU? IT'S NOT LIKE YOU HAVE ANY GROUNDS TO DETAIN ME THE WAY YOU HAVE DOCTOR MALIK.

ACTUALLY, IT'S A LOT LIKE THAT. CURT--
--DID THE PROFESSOR HAPPEN TO SHOW YOU ANY PAPERS? HOW DO WE EVEN KNOW SHE'S LEGAL?

CRAP. THEY GOT JESSIE.

I'VE GOT TO HELP HER.

JESSIE CAN HANDLE HERSELF. YOUR MISSION IS TO GET INSIDE THE RESEARCH LAB AND SECURE THE SAMPLES. DO NOT, I REPEAT, DO NOT ENGAGE TOWER'S HENCHMEN.

THE PROTOTYPE YOU'RE WEARING IS FORMIDABLE, BUT NOT ENOUGH TO TAKE OUT A SMALL ARMY OF ROOKS IN HEAVY BATTLE ARMOR.

APPLIED SCIENCES LABORATORY
14-29-36-12

SO WHAT MAKES THE STUFF IN THESE OLD MINESHAFT SAMPLES MORE VALUABLE THAN YOUR DAUGHTER, MALCOLM?

LOOK, BUDDY. I'M *NOT* GOING TO HURT YOU.
AND LET'S JUST SAY THAT THERE'S NO WAY YOU COULD POSSIBLY HURT ME.
CLK CLK
CLK CLK

CLK CLK
CLK CLK CLK CLK
BANG

ZZHHURM

SEE?

?!
THIS IS HUMMELL, REQUESTING *HEAVY* BACKUP ON THE *ROOF* OF THE SCIENCE BUILDING...

DAMMIT!

HE'S ON THE ROOF.

HNN
SHUT THAT DOWN.

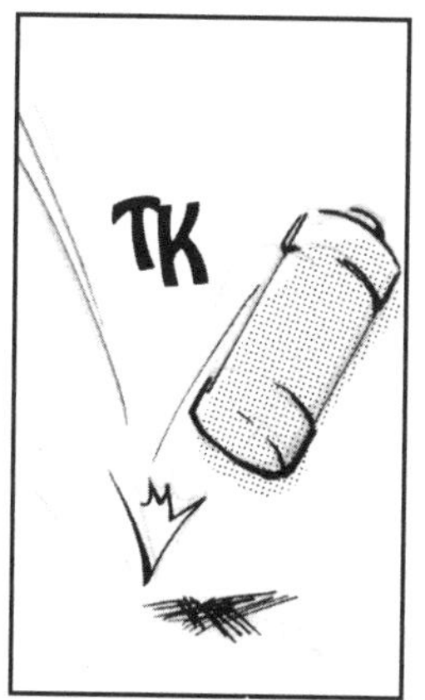
TK

kaBLAM

NINJAS? REALLY?
GOLDFIELD MINE: V.R.I.L. SAMPLES

INITIALIZING

FWIP

TAP

TRACER ACTIVATED

BEEP
WHHRRRM

ALL OF A SUDDEN, I'M STARTING TO MISS THE NINJAS.
SSSSSSSSSSS

YOU READY TO DIE, SCRUB?

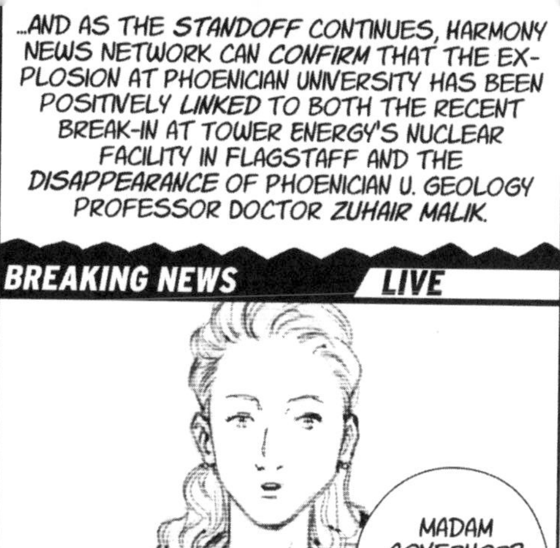
...AND AS THE STANDOFF CONTINUES, HARMONY NEWS NETWORK CAN CONFIRM THAT THE EXPLOSION AT PHOENICIAN UNIVERSITY HAS BEEN POSITIVELY LINKED TO BOTH THE RECENT BREAK-IN AT TOWER ENERGY'S NUCLEAR FACILITY IN FLAGSTAFF AND THE DISAPPEARANCE OF PHOENICIAN U. GEOLOGY PROFESSOR DOCTOR ZUHAIR MALIK.
BREAKING NEWS
LIVE
HNN
CAMPUS TERROR ATTACK IN AZ
MADAM GOVERNOR? MR. TOWER IS HERE TO SEE YOU.

...SOURCES CLOSE TO THE INVESTIGATION BELIEVE THE BOMBER -- SUSPECTED TO BE A NORTH KOREAN AGENT -- IS AN ASSOCIATE OF PAKISTANI-BORN MALIK, KNOWN TO BE A PRACTICING MUSLIM.
JONATHAN, ARE YOU WATCHING THIS? IT'S ABSOLUTELY HORRIFIC.
GOD HELP US ALL, IRIS. YOUR STATE REALLY LACKS THE MANPOWER TO PROTECT ITSELF. IT'S A GOOD THING YOUR NEW LAW GIVES YOU THE OPTION TO USE PATRIOTIC, MARKET-BASED SOLUTIONS LIKE MY WHITE ROOKS.

DEPUTIZE US TO ACT AS AN OFFICIAL TASK FORCE UNDER SB1177, AND I SWEAR WE'LL FIND THIS TERRORIST FILTH.
I CAN ONLY OFFER YOU THAT KIND OF AUTHORITY WITHIN STATE LINES, OF COURSE.

THAT'S ALL I ASK FOR, MADAM GOVERNOR.

APPARENTLY, IN THE STATE OF ARIZONA, IT'S NOW *ILLEGAL* TO LOOK LIKE ME.

TOWER'S BEEN GIVEN *CARTE BLANCHE* TO DO WHATEVER IT TAKES TO HUNT ME DOWN.

AND MEANWHILE, I'M *STILL* ON YOUR CRAZY SCAVENGER HUNT FROM HELL.

THE *MORE* ANSWERS I FIND, THE *MORE* I REALIZE I'M NOT *ASKING* THE RIGHT QUESTIONS.

WHAT DO TOWER'S MEN *WANT* WITH A PAKISTANI GEOLOGIST? WHAT'S THE CONNECTION BETWEEN MY DAD'S TECHNOLOGY AND AN ABANDONED GOLD MINE? AND *NINJAS*? WHAT'S WITH THE NINJAS?

I HAVE THE HORRIBLE FEELING I'M *ABOUT* TO FIND OUT.
THANKS FOR *NOTHING*, DAD.
NEXT CHAPTER: "THE MANIPULATOR"
HIBAKUSHA: SECRETS

AN ALIEN ON ONE'S OWN PLANET...

THE WAIT...

THE LOOK...

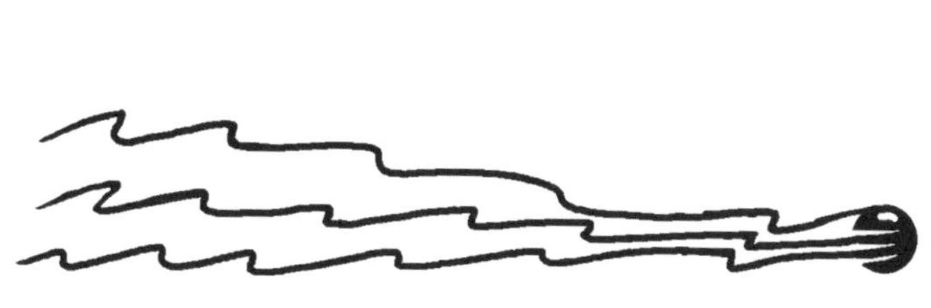

AND WORDS THAT FLY LIKE CANNONBALLS.

OUR CONFIDENCE

OUR SELF-ESTEEM.

UT WE WILL RISE AGAIN ...

STRONGER.

누드 사진!
치과
KARAOKE
순두부
약
부동산
PC 방
HAIR FASHION
WHEN WE FIRST ARRIVED HERE YEARS AGO THEY CALLED IT AN INVASION.

NOW THEY COMPLAIN WE'VE OVERRUN THEIR SCHOOLS AND THEIR BUSINESSES.
영화방
안경
노래방

THEY SAY THEY WANT TO SEND US BACK WHERE WE CAME FROM.

THEY DON'T LIKE HOW WE LOOK...

SUSHI

寿司食べる

HOW WE SMELL...

GUESS I CAN'T BLAME THEM.
FATTY TUNA
END

PERSONAL MONSTERS

STORY & ART: TRACI HONDA

CONGRATS
HOMER
THE ODYSSEY

END

EIGHTLESS

STORY: TANUJ CHOPRA
ART: ALICE MEICHI LI

They come from all
orners of the Earth...
...They all come for the
same reason:
pleasure.

They leave their cash
in our casinos.
CASINO
They dance in
our craters.

They come to feel
weightless--
to feel free.
And so they
drink our wine.

They devour
our women.
They leave a trail of refuse
everywhere they go.

They have names for us locals: "Crater Babies", "Rock Monkeys", "Lunatics".

SOMA
MEANS JOBS
UNCLE MOON
WANTS YOU!
We respond with tight plastic smiles and silence.
My parents fled war on Earth
clean toilets here on the S
of Tranquility. They ne
earned the money need
to leave this ro
But most of us who were born here don't want to...
Most of

That glowing blue ball in my sky-- it keeps me awake at night.
He never told me he'd saved his coins. I never knew he wanted to leave.
When the moon is full, I wonder... does he look up and think of me?

These clowns I interview...shallow. Boring. They all claim to be invested in this community, to want to build a new world.
But all they really want is to get in, get rich, and go home.
SOMA
STAFFIN
Tell me about yourself, Aidan. You come highly recommended.
There's nothing to tell.
You have my résum

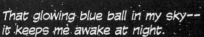

What are your goals?
To find the nearest bar. Let's get a drink.
What an unusual answer for an applicant. He reminds me of... **someone.**

I don't know why I agree. Maybe it's because, like a tourist, love leaves a trail of refuse behind. Scattered memories. Abandoned recollections.

The resemblance is...uncann

Why are you really here?
I want to blow my money before I blow my brains out.
Any suggestions?
Earthlings never talk like this.
You must be a good-luck charm. Wish I'd met you sooner.
Think of it as my standard background check...
We were married only a year when our home became a battlefield.
We survived the war... but not the religious riots that came after.
One day when I came home, the house was burnt to ashes. Utterly gone. And so were they.
These should be yours. The winnings.
Take them.

the crater club: ZERO G DANCE →
Find who you need to find. Do what you need to do.
And remember this night.
If I were to go, would I too find… nothing but ashes?
And then I think to myself: Up here, I can float. If I choose to, I could fly.
So why would I want to fall to Earth?
END

A DREAM OF FLYING

STORY: ANGELA VERONICA WONG & REINHARDT SUAREZ
PENCILS: CHRISTINE NORRIE • INKS: CRAIG YEUNG

COREY! COME LOOK, HONEY--YOUR SISTER **HART'S** ABOUT TO CATCH **THE BLACK FOX!**
I'LL **PASS,** THANKS.

EVEN ALL THE WAY OUT **HERE?**
♫ I WOULD RATHER NOT GO BACK TO THE OLD ♪ HOUSE... ♫

♪ ♫ ...WHEN YOU ♪ CYCLED BY... ♫

BACK OFF, MAN. DON'T THINK I CAN'T KICK YOUR BUTT. BECAUSE I CAN! I GO TO ***TROY ACADEMY,*** YOU KNOW? SCHOOL FOR CAPES. THIS IS JUST MY SECRET IDENTITY!
♫ HERE BEGAN ALL MY DREAMS THE SADDEST ♪ ♪ THING I'VE EVER SEEN ♫

EEEK!

OH MY GOD... IS THAT YOU, ELSTON? WOW, IT'S BEEN... AWHILE.
YEAH, APPARENTLY I'M REAL SCARY NOW.

WHAT ARE YOU DOING BACK HERE ANYWAY?
UH, NOSTALGIA, I GUESS. WANTED TO CHECK OUT THE OLD HOUSE.

THERE, CHAIN'S FIXED. WANT SOME OLD COMPANY?
SURE.

ZOOM
SO... ARE YOU STILL CRUSHING ON MY SISTER?

OH, COME ON. YOU USED TO FOLLOW HER AROUND LIKE A PUPPY.
SCREEEE!

"YOU NEVER KNEW, HOW MUCH I REALLY LIKED YOU / BECAUSE I NEVER EVEN TOLD YOU..."

THIS IS IT.
CORRECTION: *WAS* IT.

THE PAST TENSE DOES SEEM APPROPRIATE.
YEAH... TOO MANY MEMORIES.

THIS WAS OUR ROOM, REMEMBER? ME AND HART. BEFORE THE ACADEMY CALLED.

AND THEN YOU GUYS **MOVED AWAY.** THE ACADEMY TOOK YOU, TOO, DIDN'T THEY?
YEAH.

"CROSS THE CLEAR BLUE SKY AN ANGEL FLIES/ DARK HAIR, DARK EYES/ YOU WON'T FORGET-- THE STARLET"
THAT'S HART'S *THEME SONG!*

AW, MAN, I'M LATE FOR WORK!--WAIT! COREY! IT'S... IT'S MEANT TO BE *IRONIC!*
OH, PLEASE! YOU MISSED YOUR CHANCE ANYWAY. SHE'S DATING THAT JERKFACE, **WINGMAN.**

WINGMAN?

OMIGOD, IT'S TRUE? THEY'RE REALLY TOGETHER? THAT'S AWESOME! I KNEW THE HERO CHANNEL WAS FRONTING WHEN THEY SAID HE WAS DATING VENUS BUTTERFLY.
WHO'S FASTER, HART OR WING? I HEARD WING CAN HIT MACH 3, AND HART TOPS OUT AT ABOUT 1.5, BUT WING'S REALLY A SPRINTER--IF IT WERE CROSS-COUNTRY OR ROUND-THE-WORLD HE'D BE TOAST--

WAIT. YOU'RE... A FAN?
NOT JUST HART AND WINGMAN. I LOVE ALL THE SKYLINE HEROES--AIRSTRIKE, CLOUDBERRY. FLYING--IT'S MY DREAM POWER, YOU KNOW? SO I COULD JUST FLY AWAY FROM MY STUPID DRUNK DAD AND MY STUPID DUMB LIFE.
LIKE YOU GUYS DID...LIKE MY MOM DID.

SHE TOOK OFF LAST YEAR. MARRIED SOME BUSINESS BIG SHOT. IT'S GROSS.

EVERYBODY'S GROSS! EVERYONE LOVES WINNERS, RIGHT? WELL, WHAT ABOUT THE REST OF US?
LIKE... OH, LOOK AT HART, SHE'S SO AWESOME. "WHY CAN'T YOU MOVE MOUNTAINS WITH YOUR MIND, COREY? WHY AREN'T YOU DOING PH.D.-LEVEL CHEMISTRY WORK, WHY AREN'T YOU POPULAR, WHY AREN'T YOU A CHEERLEADER? WHY CAN'T YOU FLY?"

YOU CAN'T FLY?
NOT REALLY. NO.

BOOOM

DID YOU DO THAT?
...YEAH.
DID YOU KNOW YOU COULD DO THAT?
NO. I MEAN, HART CAN'T DO THAT.

YOU KNOW I MEANT THE *FORCE FIELD,* RIGHT?
YOU DORK.

OH MAN, I *REALLY* GOTTA GET TO WORK.
I SHOULD HEAD HOME.
RIGHT-- I NEARLY FORGOT.
HAPPY BIRTHDAY.

YOU *KNOW* IT'S MY BIRTHDAY?
OF COURSE.
HEY, IF YOU DON
HAVE TO HEAD B
RIGHT AWAY, CO
WITH ME. I'LL TRE
YOU TO A SHAK

GUESS WE'RE WALKING.
NOT LIKE WE CAN FLY.

FLYING'S *OVERRATED.*

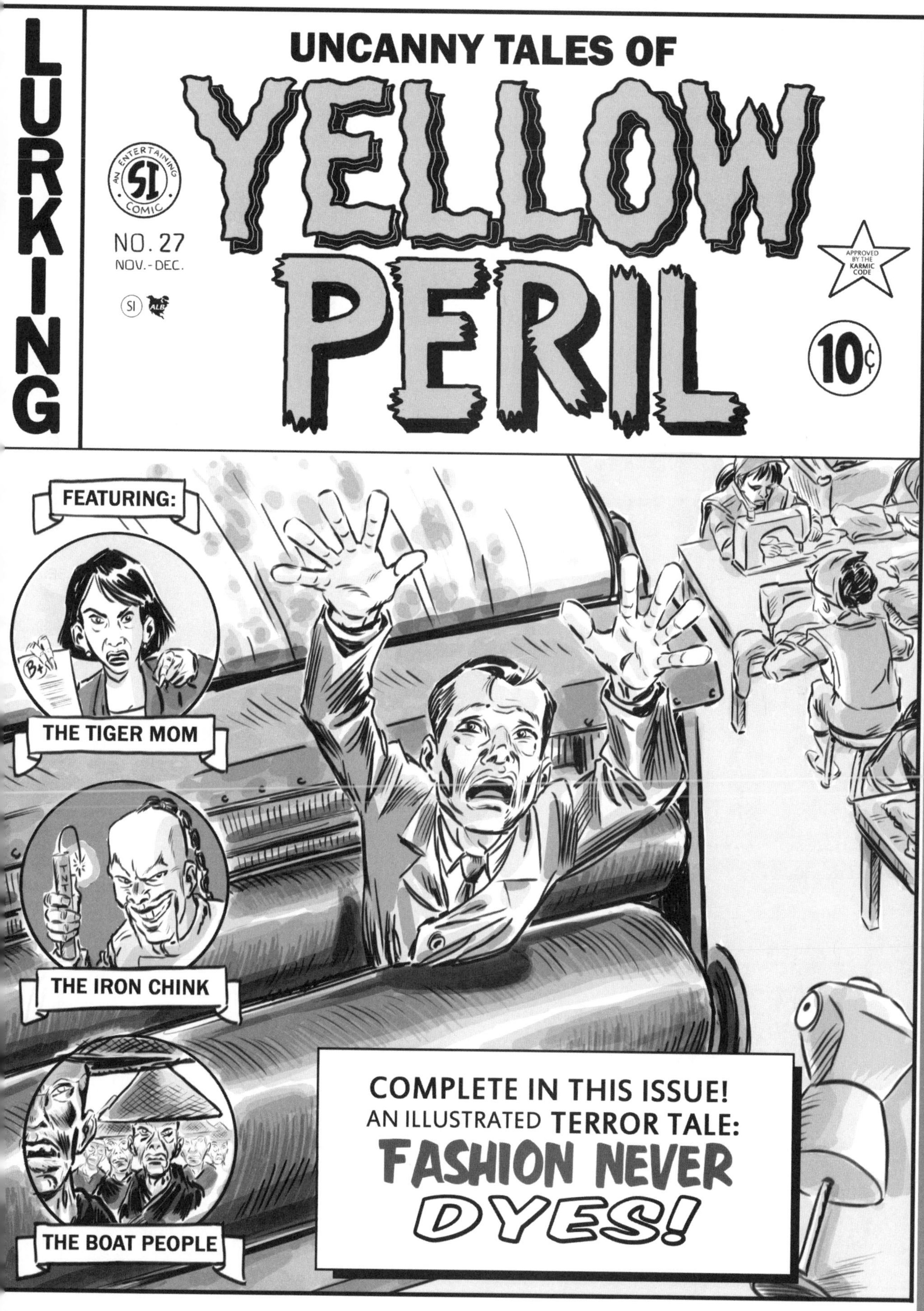

FEATURING:

THE TIGER MOM

THE IRON CHINK

THE BOAT PEOPLE

COMPLETE IN THIS ISSUE!
AN ILLUSTRATED TERROR TALE:
FASHION NEVER DYES!

STORY: JAMIE FORD
ART: A.L. BAROZA

TOMMY RUI HAS GRACIOUSLY OPENED HIS DOORS TO HIS **BEATEN RIVALS,** BECAUSE NO ONE CAN COMPETE WITH HIS CLOTHING EMPIRE–**NO ONE!**

PLEASE, **MR. RUI!** YOU CAN'T KEEP SELLING YOUR FASHIONS FOR **HALF** OUR PRICES.
AND YOUR **SLAVE-LABOR** TACTICS–THEY'LL PUT US OUT OF BUSINESS!

GENTLEMEN, YOU **WOUND** ME! MY DESIGNS ARE FAIRLY PRICED.
AND I GRACE THESE **HARD-WORKING** PEOPLE WITH JOBS...

YOU'RE MERELY **JEALOUS** OF MY TRUE **GREATNESS**–MY DESIGNS, MY UNPARALLELED SENSE OF **STYLE.** NOW **GET OUT**–BEFORE I HAVE YOU **THROWN OUT!**

ENRAGED, TOMMY RUI VOWS TO CRUSH WHAT REMAINS OF HIS COMPETITION.
I'LL **BLOODY WELL** SHOW THEM. JUST WAIT TILL THEY SEE MY SPRING-SUMMER **ORIGINALS.**
MY COLLECTION WILL BE THE **SENSATION OF SEVENTH AVENUE!**

NO! NO! **I'M CAUGHT!**

SOMEBODY! ANYBODY! HELP ME! **YAAAAAAAAA!**

TOMMY
(GASP!) HOW DOES HE **DO IT?**
(SOB) I'M **DYING** TO KNOW.
I GUESS THAT
WHAT HAPPEN
...WHEN **FASHI**
IS IN YOUR
BLOOD!
TOMMY

"THERE IS A CROSS-SECTION OF INDIVIDUALS AND OFFSPRING THAT HAVE SURVIVED THE ATOMIC BOMBS OF HIROSHIMA AND NAGASAKI--LITERALLY TRANSLATING INTO "EXPLOSION-AFFECTED PEOPLE", THEY ARE KNOWN AS...THE HIBAKUSHA."
KYOTO, JAPAN.
"Dear Dad: I know you're wondering where I am and what I'm doing, and I can't tell you. But all I know is... it just feels right."

don't know why we couldn't ess what the US government's nda was for us when they had pulling apart tanks..."*
YUCCA FLATS, NV--AREA 52, ATOMIC PROGENY DIVISION
YOW! EASY, KAT!!
*AS SEEN IN SECRET IDENTITIES

ou always said there was no 'silver lining' the bombing. Well, our teacher, Mishira, ieves that too."
LOCKE!
AGHHH!

"But our breakout came at the expense of many."
RYAN... THE...

THE TRUTH IS--HERE.
DEPARTMENT OF ... UNITED STATES OF AM...
THEIR MEDICS WILL TREAT HIM. NOW COME--WE MUST MAKE HASTE.
"...We've done amazing things in the six months we've been here."
RYAN, ALL FLAMES ABSORBED!
...AND LAST OF THE DEBRIS FLYIN' OUT NOW.
"You'd be so proud."
"The researchers here have discovered ways to boost..."
CONDITION: NORMAL
147
"...and control our abilities."
148
YOUR HYPEREPINEPHR LEVELS ARE LOOKI GOOD, RYAN-SA

AIR MAIL
ASA S
347 BR
SACR
"As always, I hope you're well and promise to send for you soon. Love, Ryan."
POST
ZZSHHT!
MISH
DIRECTOR
<AH, MISHIRA-DONO IS NOT CURRENTLY PRESENT!>
<IS THERE SOMETHING I MIGHT HELP YOU WITH?>
LISTEN CAREFULLY, AS I'M ONLY GOING TO ASK THIS ONCE...

HMM, LEMME GUESS. YOU'RE DEPRESSED ABOUT THE POUNDS YOU'VE GAINED SINCE LEARNING HOW TO REPEL GRAVITY AND FLYING AROUND EVERYWHERE.
OH COME ON, YOU'LL LOSE THE CHUB. JUST STOP BEING SO LAZY AND WALK ONCE IN AWHILE.
I MEAN, OUR REGULATORS ALONE WEIGH LIKE AN EXTRA TEN POUNDS.
DICE, WHAT'S WRONG?
"I WAS WALKING DOWN CENTRAL CORRIDOR AT THE COMPLEX..."
"REALLY? 'WALKING'?"
"FLOATING, WHATEVER...ANYWAY, MISHIRA-SENSEI WAS THERE LOOKING ALL SERIOUS."
"HE SAID THE JAPANESE SQUAD APPREHENDED A KNOWN BOMB MAKER."
"THEY LOCATED THE BOMB BUT NEEDED THE DEACTIVATION CODE."
"MISHIRA SAID WE HAD THREE MINUTES BEFORE IT WOULD DETONATE--RIGHT IN THE HEART OF DOWNTOWN TOKYO."
"YIKES...SO WHAT'D YOU DO?"
"I...HELPED."
WAIT, WHAT IS HE DOING?
DAISUKE, HE'S STALLING...

NO...PLEASE! I'LL TELL YOU WHATEVER YOU WANT...!
HE'S TOLD US NOTHING FOR THE LAST HOUR...
UGH--
AGH!! 14-29-36-12!!!
CRAACKK
KAT--I DID THE RIGHT THING, RIGHT? I SAVED ALL THOSE PEOPLE...
ARE YOU KIDDING? WE LEFT THE PROGENY PROGRAM TO GET AWAY FROM THAT KIND OF STUFF.
COME ON...
WE GOTTA GO FIND RYAN."
PLEASE, I WAS JUST DOING WHAT I WAS TOLD!
BY WHO?!?
M...M... MISHIRA-DONO...
KHOOOM!!
YOU LIE!!

"THE TRUTH IS--HERE."
UGGH!
OH BOY.
FAP!
FAP!
FAP!
FAP!
HIM!>

SHREEN
WHAT THE--

PHOENICIAN UNIVERSITY, ARIZONA
<HOW DID YOU KNOW HE WOULD DO IT?>
14-29-36-12
ACCESS GRANTED
TOWER INDUSTRIES
GOLDFIELD MINE V.R.I.L. SAMPLES
GOLDFIELD MINE V.R.I.L. SAMPLES

<DESPITE THE EVER-CHANGING VARIABLES SINCE THIS PROJECT INCEPTION, ONE THING HAS ALWA REMAINED CONSTANT...>

<..."LOST SOULS WILL ALWAYS SEEK DIRECTION.">
DICE. LET'S GO!

"I JUST DISCOVERED A DIRTY LITTLE 75-YEAR-OLD SECRET."
TRINITY TEST REPORT
July 16, 1945
Henry Dewolf Smith
CLK
"I'VE ALREADY REWOUND AND PLAYED IT TWICE."
"BEFORE, EVERYTHING WAS SO CLEAR..."
RYAN! WAIT UP!
AFTER STUDYING THIS REPORT ON THE AMERICAN'S ATOMIC TESTS...
"...WHO TO FOLLOW..."
TRINITY TEST REPORT
July 16, 1945
Henry Dewolf Smith
MISHIRA
ENGLISH
...I FEAR THE EMPIRE MAY SOON WITNESS ITS MASSIVE DESTRUCTIVE CAPACITY FIRSTHAND.
"...AND WHO TO BLAME."
MISHIRA
HOWEVER, FROM THIS DISASTER MAY SPRING HOPE--AND ULTIMATELY, VICTORY.
IT SEEMS THAT OUR UNIT 731'S ENERGON AMPLIFICATION EXPERIMENTS COUPLED WITH THE REICH'S MUTAGENICS RESEARCH MAY FINALLY BEAR FRUIT.
THERE YOU ARE! HOLY--WHAT ARE YOU DOING?!
HEY, THAT DUDE LOOKS LIKE A REALLY YOUNG...
<AS PLANNED, SHADOWTHIEF, I WILL MEET YOU AND THE BURIRU IN TROY CITY-->
<MISHIRA-SAN! THERE'S BEEN A BREACH AT THE RADIO TOWER!>

WHILE THE SAMPLES OF THE BURIRU SHARED BY OUR GERMAN FRIENDS YIELDED UNSTABLE RESULTS, WHEN PROPERLY PREPARED IN SUCH CONTAINERS...
73 部隊
... AND SUFFUSED WITH SUFFICIEN ENERGY, THE BURIRU CAN BE UTILIZ TO CONTROL MUTAGENIC ACTIVITY EMBEDDING THE POTENTIAL FOR LIMITLESS, METAHUMAN POWER.
...IN THOSE THAT SURVIVE OR IN THEIR DESCENDANTS. THESE CHILDREN OF THE FUTURE MIGHT ONE DAY HAVE...
"...THE STRENGTH OF A HUNDRED MEN..."
"...THE ABILITY TO RIDE THE WINDS..."
"...OR TO HARNESS THE HEART OF THE RISING SUN ITSELF."
ALTHOUGH IT IS CERTAIN THIS WAR IS LOST, OUR EMPEROR HAS DECREED THAT WE WILL, LIKE THE PHOENIX, EMBRACE THE FLAMES, SEEKING REBIRTH THROUGH A FUTURE GENERATION.
A GENERATION THAT WILL STRIKE BACK AT OUR ENEMIES WITH A FORCE A THOUSAND TIMES MORE POTENT THAN ANY THE WORLD HAS SEEN.
THESE PODS CONTAINING THE BURIRU MATRIX WILL BE PLACED IN OUR NATION'S EPICENTERS WHERE ATOMIC TARGETING IS MOST LIKELY...
TRUNCATED
WE ALL KNOW THE ENDING, DON'T WE?
TKT
YOU COULD HAVE EVACUATED THOSE CITIES!

YOU COULD HAVE SAVED OUR FAMILIES--ALL OUR SHATTERED LIVES-- ARGGH!!!
ZSST
I JUST INCREASED YOUR REGULATOR'S HYPEREPINEPHRINE RELEASE BY A FACTOR OF TEN.
UGHH!
STAND DOWN OR I MAKE IT A THOUSAND. AND YOU CAN WATCH AS HIS BODY TEARS ITSELF APART.
YOU DIDN'T THINK I'D LET AN ANIMAL LIKE YOU INTO MY COMPOUND WITHOUT A LEASH, DID YOU?
YOU WERE ALL BROUGHT HERE IN HOPES OF CORRECTING YOUR MINDS AND WINNING YOUR HEARTS. BUT FAILING THAT...
...WE COULD AT LEAST RECOVER YOUR BLOOD.
BLOOD SUFFUSED WITH THE BURIRU MATRIX--
--BLOOD FROM WHICH THAT PRECIOUS GOLDEN SUBSTANCE COULD BE PAINSTAKINGLY EXTRACTED TO USE ON MORE AMENABLE SUBJECTS.
BUT THANKS TO DAISUKE-KUN, WE HAVE ACCESS TO ENOUGH OF THE BURIRU TO EXECUTE THE EMPEROR'S PLAN IMMEDIATELY.
AND THAT MEANS NOTHING PREVENTS US FROM EXECUTING ALL OF YOU.

SUCH A WASTE. BUT THE EMPEROR AND I NEVER FORESAW THE TAINTED INFLUENCES OF... AMERICAN ASSIMILATION.
...KEEP...TALKING...
CRKKKK
IS EVERYTHING READY TO BE RELEASED UPON TROY?
YES, MISHIRA-DONO.
THE EMPEROR AND I WILL AWAIT IN THE SHUTTLE. FINISH THEM QUICKLY.
AHH--
--HGHH!
FWOOM!!
THWAAAP
<SQUID-KUN!!>
HMPH. YOU THROW LIKE AN AME-KOH.
DON'T KNOW WHAT THAT MEANS, SQUID-- BUT TELL ME, HOW DO I...

...HIT!?!
SSSSSooo
KRAKK!
SSSSSS...
"NOT BAD," I'D SAY.
WAIT--THAT WAS RHETORICAL, RIGHT?
HA! LEARNED THIS YESTERDAY. NOW LET'S ALL GO FOR...
BRATATATATATATAT
TINK
TINK
TINK
TINK
TINK

SLAMMMM!
...A RIDE!
BOOM!
COME ON. WE GOTTA STOP MISHIRA!
THAT'S THE "SHUTTLE"?
IS HE HEADED TO AMERICA, OR THE...
DICE, HOW FAST CAN YOU FLY THESE DAYS?
LET'S FIND OUT.
...EEED!
FWOOOOSHHH
...MOON... WOOAAH!
OOOF!
I FEEL THE NEED, THE NEED FOR SP...
KRRRRRROOOMM!!
LAST CHAPTER: THE BIG FINALE
THE SEALING

PUSH

STORY: JENNIFER S. FANG • PENCILS: ACE CONTINUADO • INKS: JULIAN SAN JUAN

"...THE SINGLE WORST MASS MURDERER IN AMERICAN HISTORY IS GONNA WALK OUT OF THAT ROOM TONIGHT A FREE MAN."
LELAND, IS IT? SORRY TO KEEP YOU WAITING. WOULD YOU LIKE SOME WATER?
YES, THANK YOU. IT'S QUITE WARM IN HERE.
BY LAW, I HAVE TO INFORM YOU THAT YOU'RE BEING RECORDED, AND THAT EVERYTHING YOU SAY MAY BE USED AGAINST YOU IN A COURT OF LAW. ARE YOU COMFORTABLE WITH THAT?
I WOULD EXPECT NOTHING LESS.
ALL RIGHT, LELAND--YOU'RE FINE IF I CALL YOU LELAND?--LET'S HAVE A LOOK. HMM...NO PRIORS. NOT EVEN A PARKING TICKET. ACADEMIC BOWL CHAMPION IN HIGH SCHOOL, NATIONAL MERIT SCHOLAR, MADE THE DEAN'S LIST IN ORGANIC CHEMISTRY.
SOUNDS LIKE YOU MIGHT'VE BEEN QUITE THE ON-CAMPUS CELEBRITY...
OH, I'M SURE YOU WOULDN'T HAVE NOTICED ME.
"SO, LELAND, TELL ME...
9:20 A.M.
POLICE
"...HOW DID A SMART KID LIKE YOU END UP IN A MESS LIKE THIS?"

THE EGGHEADS SAY IT WAS SOME KIND OF CHEMICAL WEAPON. FILLED THE SPORTS COMPLEX WITH HYDROCHLORIC ACID GAS-- LITERALLY MELTED THE FLESH OFF OF EVERYONE IN THE KILL ZONE.
EVERYONE, THAT IS, EXCEPT YOU. STRANGE, ISN'T IT?
11:46 A.M.
AN INVISIBLE COAT OF DEATH. INESCAPABLE. IMPOSSIBLE TO WASH OFF.
AND, WELL, YOU'VE SEEN THE PICTURES...
THIS ISN'T ONE OF YOUR LITTLE SCIENCE EXPERIMENTS, YOU SICK MONSTER. THOSE WERE REAL PEOPLE...
...MOTHERS. INFANTS. WHY WOULD YOU--
HYDROGEN CHLORIDE.
WHAT?
THE GAS WAS HYDROGEN CHLORIDE. NORMALLY HARMLESS. BUT ADD WATER-- PERSPIRATION OR SALIVA WILL DO-- AND IT IS CONVERTED INTO HYDROCHLORIC ACID.
AH, THE MILLION-DOLLAR QUESTION: WHY? NO CURIOSITY ABOUT HOW.
EVERYONE ALWAYS WANTS TO KNOW WHY.
GACY
GACY
DID YOU KNOW THAT AFTER JOHN WAYNE GACY DIED, SCIENTISTS REMOVED HIS BRAIN HOPING TO UNCOVER THE ABNORMALITY THAT TURNED HIM INTO A MURDERER?
ALL THEY FOUND WAS A PERFECTLY AVERAGE, ORDINARY BRAIN.
SOME PEOPLE ARE JUST EVIL. AND WHEN THEY DO EVIL THINGS, SOMEONE HAS TO STOP THEM. SOMEONE LIKE ME.
"NO CHILD IS BORN A VILLAIN.
11:48 A.M.
1992
"AND NO CHILD IS BORN A HERO.
"OUR EXPERIENCES SHAPE US INTO THE MEN WE BECOME.
"BUT EVEN THAT'S TOO SIMPLE AN EXPLANATION, ISN'T IT?"

"ALL OF US ARE CAPABLE OF ORDINARY DEEDS. TRIVIAL GOOD. PETTY EVIL.
"BUT THERE ARE A RARE FEW WHOM FATE GIVES THE CHANCE TO BE EXTRAORDINARY.
2001
2002
SSSSSSSSSSS
KA-BOOOM!
"FOR THOSE FEW, ALL IT TAKES IS A CATALYST A LITTLE...PUSH."
TELL ME, DO YOU THINK OF YOURSELF AS EXTRAORDINARY? IS THAT WHAT MOTIVATES YOU TO PUT ON THAT SKIN-TIGHT SPANDEX AND THAT RIDICULOUS CAPE?
I PROTECT PEOPLE. FROM PEOPLE LIKE YOU.
BUT THERE WILL ALWAYS BE MORE EVIL IN THE WORLD THAN YOU COULD EVER HOPE TO STOP.
11:49 A.M.

I'VE SAVED MORE LIVES THAN YOU CAN COUNT! THEY NEED ME OUT THERE!
HUNGER, WAR, POVERTY, DISEASE--ALL OF THESE KILL MORE PEOPLE DAILY THAN A HUNDRED PEOPLE LIKE ME.
SO TELL ME, ADAM, IS IT REALLY US WHO NEED YOU?
HOW DO YOU KNOW MY NAME?
OH, THERE WAS A TIME WHEN I WAS LIKE THEM. WHEN I WOULD'VE GIVEN ANYTHING TO HAVE YOUR LIFE--SON OF A WAR HERO, STAR ATHLETE, GOLDEN BOY. AND THEN I STOPPED MYSELF AND ASKED: WHY WOULD I WANT TO?
AFTER ALL, THE SAME ACCIDENT THAT GAVE YOU THE STRENGTH TO PUNCH THROUGH STEEL DID NOTHING TO BOOST YOUR IQ.
SHUT UP.
YOU'RE NOTHING BUT A CHILD IN A TITAN'S BODY PLAYING AT BEING A HERO, WHO THINKS HE CAN SAVE US FROM ALL THE EVIL THAT MEN DO ARMED WITH NOTHING MORE THAN A GOOD RIGHT HOOK.
SHUT UP.
WHEN PUSH COMES TO SHOVE, ADAM, YOU'RE NO BETTER THAN THE REST OF US.
SHUT UP! SHUT UP! SHUT UP!
DAMN!

DO YOU KNOW WHY I CHOSE TO STUDY CHEMISTRY?
BECAUSE EVERY MOLECULE IN THE UNIVERSE CARRIES THE POTENTIAL TO BECOME SOMETHING ELSE. ALMOST ANYTHING ELSE.
ALL YOU NEED TO KNOW IS WHERE TO GIVE THE RIGHT TINY LITTLE PUSH.
11:52 A.M.
YOU SEE, THAT'S WHAT THE ACCIDENT GAVE ME.
9:11 A.M.
"YOUR FISTS CAN DEMOLISH A MOUNTAIN.
"BUT WITH A SINGLE FINGER I CAN REMAKE THE WORLD.
ADAM, DID YOU KNOW THAT EVERY CELL IN YOUR BODY HAS PROGRAMMED WITHIN IT THE POTENTIAL TO COMMIT SUICIDE?
11:52 A.M.
"IT'S AN ELEGANT LITTLE BIOCHEMICAL PROCESS CALLED APOPTOSIS."

HAVE YOU NOTICED, ADAM, A LITTLE ITCH IN YOUR HAND? A TIGHTNESS SPREADING IN YOUR CHEST?
"IS YOUR HEART STRUGGLING TO BEAT?
IRONIC, ISN'T IT, ADAM? A TINY PUFF OF CALCIUM--AND EVEN THE MIGHTIEST OF THE MIGHTY WILL FALL.
ALL THAT POWER. AND YET I KILLED YOU WHEN YOU HANDED ME THAT GLASS OF WATER.
YOU ASKED ME, WHY WOULD I MURDER HUNDREDS OF INNOCENTS?
WAS IT TO GET YOUR NOTICE? HARDLY.
IT WOULD HAVE TAKEN MUCH LESS THAN THIS TO GET YOUR ATTENTION, ADAM. A CRY IN THE NIGHT, A KITTEN IN A TREE.
"THIS WAS NEVER ABOUT YOU.
"YOU'RE JUST A MEANS TO AN END.
REC
"THIS WAS ALWAYS ABOUT THEM."

11:57 A.M.
REC •
"THEY'LL WATCH, STUDY AND DISSECT THIS--BECAUSE THEY'LL WANT TO KNOW WHY.
"EVERYONE ALWAYS WANTS TO KNOW WHY.
"AND WHEN THEY DO, THEY'LL SEE YOU AS YOU TRULY ARE: WEAK. EMPTY. IMPERFECT. UNWORTHY.
"BY SHOWING THEM THIS TRUTH, I'M SAVING THEM IN A WAY YOU NEVER COULD.
"LIKE A MOTHER BIRD, WHO IN ALL HER CRUEL KINDNESS BRINGS HER CHICKS TO THE EDGE OF THE NEST AND GIVES THEM A PUSH...
"...SO THAT THEY MIGHT TAKE WING ON THEIR OWN.
11:59 A.M.
"OH, AND ONE MORE THING, ADAM:
A CHEMICAL REACTION."
CLICK

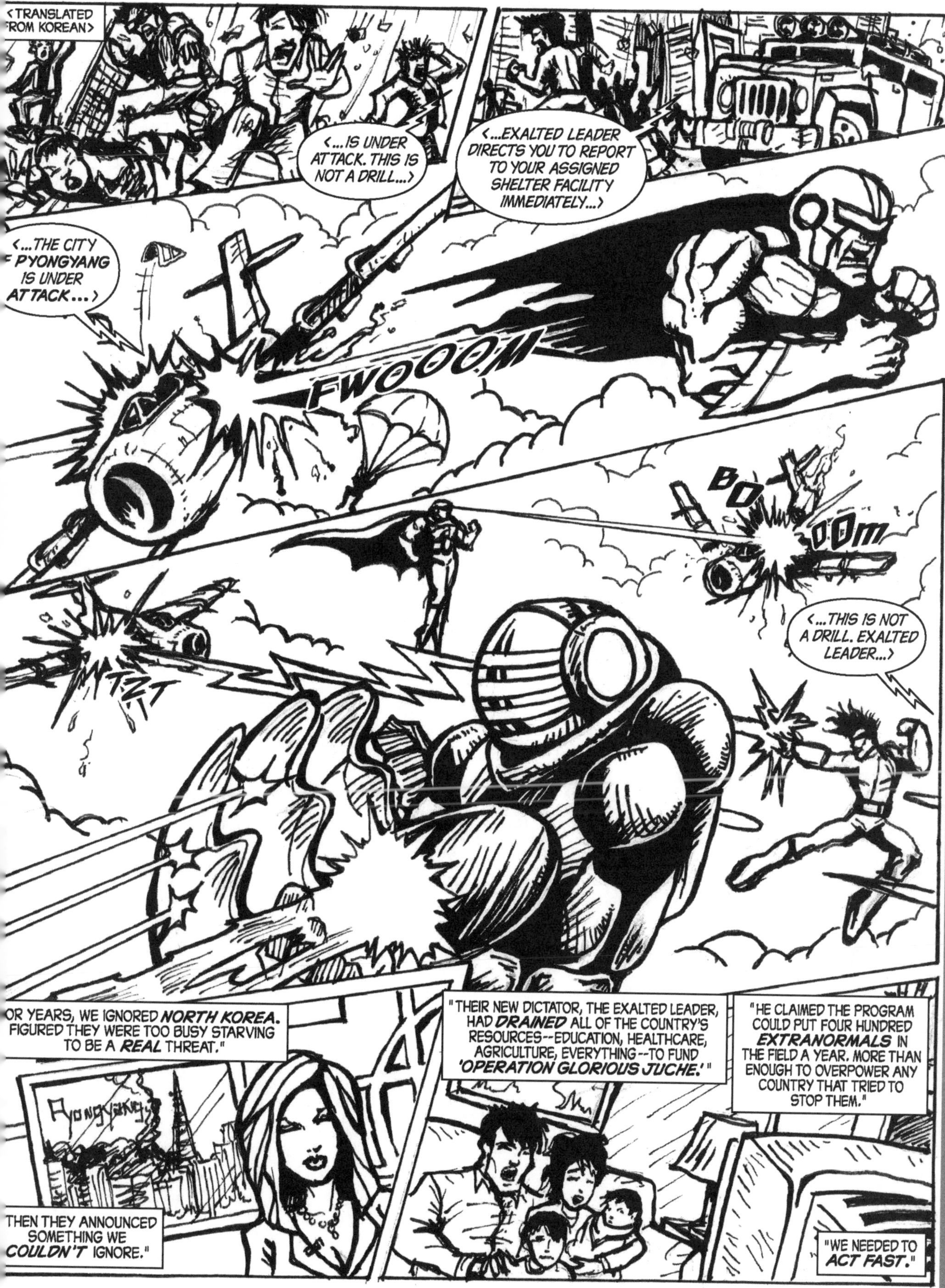
<TRANSLATED FROM KOREAN>
<...IS UNDER ATTACK. THIS IS NOT A DRILL...>
<...EXALTED LEADER DIRECTS YOU TO REPORT TO YOUR ASSIGNED SHELTER FACILITY IMMEDIATELY...>
<...THE CITY F PYONGYANG IS UNDER ATTACK...>
FWOOOM
BOOOM
<...THIS IS NOT A DRILL. EXALTED LEADER...>
TZT
OR YEARS, WE IGNORED NORTH KOREA. FIGURED THEY WERE TOO BUSY STARVING TO BE A REAL THREAT."
PYONGYANG
THEN THEY ANNOUNCED SOMETHING WE COULDN'T IGNORE."
"THEIR NEW DICTATOR, THE EXALTED LEADER, HAD DRAINED ALL OF THE COUNTRY'S RESOURCES--EDUCATION, HEALTHCARE, AGRICULTURE, EVERYTHING--TO FUND 'OPERATION GLORIOUS JUCHE.'"
"HE CLAIMED THE PROGRAM COULD PUT FOUR HUNDRED EXTRANORMALS IN THE FIELD A YEAR. MORE THAN ENOUGH TO OVERPOWER ANY COUNTRY THAT TRIED TO STOP THEM."
"WE NEEDED TO ACT FAST."

"SO WE DID."
"THEY CALL ME--
SENTINEL."
ARMISTICE
KID
LIGHTNING
DIAMOND
JACK
QUEEN
FLAGSTAFF
"THE GOLDEN GUILD.
AND OUR OWN 'EXALTED
LEADER,' FLAGSTAFF..."
IF WE CAN'T FIND THIS
UNDERGROUND LAB,
WE WILL LOSE THIS WAR.
UNDERSTAND?
"FAILURE IS NOT
AN OPTION."
"LISTENING TO HIM, YOU
WOULDN'T KNOW THAT THE
SIX OF US HAD JUST SENT
AN ENTIRE COUNTRY BACK
TO THE STONE AGE."
"DAYS GO BY."
"WE SPEND MOST OF OUR TIME
DOING DAMAGE CONTROL;
PUTTING DOWN WHAT
PASSES FOR RESISTANCE."
"I KEEP THINKING: THIS IS A COUNTRY
THREATENING TO TAKE ON THE WORLD?"
"THE DAYS TURN INTO WEEKS. STILL
NO TRACE OF WHAT WE CAME
TO FIND. NO SECRET COMPLEX.
NO UNDERGROUND LAB."
"MAYBE IT'S A MYTH, LIKE
ATLANTIS. LIKE SHANGRI-LA."

"BUT WE KEEP SEARCHING. DETERMINED TO PROVE OURSELVES RIGHT."
"BECAUSE, REALLY..."
"...WHAT CHOICE DO WE HAVE?"
<THERE IS NO REASON FOR YOU TO DO THIS! YOU OWE THEM NOTHING!>
<I CANNOT DISHONOR MY COUNTRY ANY MORE THAN I ALREADY HAVE.>
<BAD ENOUGH WHAT THESE AMERICAN "HEROES" HAVE DONE.>
<I WON'T LEAVE YOU!>
<PLEASE... I AM THE ONLY ONE WHO CAN MAKE THIS RIGHT. WHEN I FINISH, I WILL JOIN YOU.>
<TAKE THE TRAIN. THE LINES NO LONGER WORK, BUT PEOPLE ARE WALKING THE TRACKS. IT'S SAFER UNDERGROUND—MANY HAVE ALREADY CROSSED OVER.>
<BUT WHAT IF I'M CAUGHT?>
<YOU WON'T BE. AND WHEN YOU ESCAPE, THINK OF OUR HOMELAND WITH PRIDE—ITS HONOR RIGHTFULLY RESTORED.>
<NOW PLEASE, YOU'VE WASTED TOO MUCH TIME...>
<...I WILL JOIN YOU SOON.>
<HANG TIGHT, I'LL HAVE YOU OUT IN A SECOND.>
"I REMIND MYSELF THAT, DESPITE EVERYTHING, WE'RE HERE AS LIBERATORS. AND YET..."

"...OUR ROLE HERE IS CONSTANTLY... MISINTERPRETED."
<BETTER TO HAVE DIED THAN BEEN SAVED BY FILTH LIKE YOU! LOOK AT WHAT YOU'VE DONE TO THOSE OF YOUR OWN BLOOD! AND YET YOU THINK WE OWE YOU THANKS?>
<BUT WE'RE HERE TO HELP!>
IT'S ALL JUST A JOKE, ISN'T IT?
YO SEN, YOU LUCKY YOU GOT SOMEONE WATCHING YOUR BACK...
YOU OKAY?
THERE'S NO PROGRAM. WE'VE BEEN WASTING OUR TIME-- WASTED AN ENTIRE COUNTRY--FOOLING OURSELVES INTO THINKING WE'VE DONE THE RIGHT THING.
HEADS UP, GUYS, WE HAVE A LEAD.
WE ROUNDED UP A BUNCH OF NKS TRYING TO ESCAPE TO THE SOUTH THROUGH THE TUBES. DID A ROUTINE MIND-SCAN AND ONE OF THEM PUT UP QUITE THE FIGHT, FOR ALL THE GOOD IT DID HER.
I KNOW IT DON'T LOOK GOOD, SEN; BUT YOU GOTTA REMIND YOURSELF-- WE'RE THE GOOD GUYS HERE.
GOT THE LOCATION OF A SECRET BUNKER. WE THINK THIS IS IT. THE TWO OF YOU CAN GET THERE FASTER THAN ANY OF US. PIPING THE COORDINATES TO YOU NOW.

ON IT, QUEENIE.
SEN, YOU READY?
ZZZERG
YOU! STOP!
<SIR, PLEASE STEP AWAY FROM THAT CONSOLE. WE WILL DO WHAT WE NEED TO IN ORDER TO STOP YOU. YOUR LIFE IS IN JEOPARDY.>
VOOOOOOOOOOOOOOOOM
<THERE ARE SOME THINGS THAT ARE MORE IMPORTANT THAN LIFE.>
NO! ROBERT, I COULD HAVE TELEPORTED AND STOPPED HIM!
SORRY, SEN, I COULDN'T TAKE THE CHANCE.

WHAT DOES IT SAY?
IT SAYS... SELF-DESTRUCT SYSTEM ABORTED. HE WASN'T TRYING TO ACTIVATE THE LAB. HE WAS TRYING TO DESTROY IT.
SELF DESTRUCT
ABORTED
"TURNS OUT IT WAS ALL POSTURING. THERE WAS NO PROGRAM. THERE WAS NEVER A PROGRAM. THE MONEY, ALONG WITH EXALTED LEADER, WAS ALREADY LONG GONE."
"FLAGSTAFF TELLS US WE DIDN'T HAVE A CHOICE. THE STAKES WERE TOO HIGH. IF NORTH KOREA HAD LAUNCHED THE PROGRAM, WE WOULD HAVE BEEN CATAPULTED INTO A WORLD WAR."
S12
"OFFICIALLY, THE WORLD AGREES. WE DID THE RIGHT THING."
"I WANT TO BELIEVE THIS IS TRUE."
END

THE MERCIFUL

GREAT ONE, *THE VISITORS* ARE HERE.

SEND FOR THEM.
"WHAT BROUGHT US TO THIS FATE?"

STORY: REN HSIE
ART: BRYAN LE

"I WAS JUST A BOY WHEN THE VISITORS FIRST ARRIVED IN THEIR SPLENDID SHIPS..."
"...LED BY A GREAT M
WITH GOLDEN HAI
"THEY OFFERED TO SHARE WITH US GREAT KNOWLEDGE. TO GIVE US WONDERFUL THINGS."
"IN RETURN, ALL THEY ASKED FOR WAS THE ROCKS BENEATH OUR FEET. OUR ELDERS THOUGHT THEY MUST BE FOOLS TO STRIKE SUCH A BARGAIN."
"IT SOON BECAME CLEAR THAT WE WERE THE FOOLS. THEY DESPOILED OUR LAND. ENSLAVED OUR PEOPLE-- NOT WITH WEAPONS, BUT WITH THE PROMISE OF SOFT LUXURIES."
"MEN WHO ONCE MIGHT HAVE GROWN INTO GREAT WARRIORS INSTEAD WENT TO WORK IN THEIR MINES."
"MANY HAD ACCIDENTS; THE LUCKY ONES DIE
THE UNLUCKY BECAME DEPENDENT ON THE VISITO
STRANGE MEDICINE TO DULL THEIR PAIN."
"AS MY GENERATION REACHED ADULTHOOD, WATCHING WHAT BEFELL OUR FATHERS AND MOTHERS, WE FELT WE NO LONGER HAD A CHOICE."
"AND SO, WE ROSE IN REBELLION."
"IT WAS TIME TO TAKE BACK OUR LAND."
"OUR LIVES."

"WE FACED LITTLE RESISTANCE.
"BUT THEN WE HAD TO DECIDE WHAT WE WOULD DO WITH THEM. SHOULD WE LET THEM RETURN TO THE STARS?
"OR SHOULD WE SIMPLY PUT AN END TO THEIR THREAT ONCE AND FOR ALL?
"MY PEOPLE HAD CHOSEN ME TO LEAD THEM BECAUSE OF MY SKILLS IN BATTLE.
"SO IT WAS TO THEIR GREAT SURPRISE THAT I ADVISED WE LET THE VISITORS GO, NEVER TO RETURN.
"THEY CALLED ME 'THE MERCIFUL ONE.'
"BUT THE MAN WITH GOLDEN HAIR WOULD RETURN... USING PROPAGANDA OF OUR SAVAGE TREACHERY TO BUILD AN ARMY."

MERCIFUL ONE, THE VISITORS SAY THAT THE TREATY-- IT MUST BE SIGNED.
"THEY BELIEVE THAT IF I SIGN THIS, IT WILL END..."
"THEY BELIEVED THAT IN A FLASH OUR UPRISING HAD BEEN PUT DOWN AND OUR PLANET CONQUERED ONCE MORE."
"BUT THE REVOLUTION ONLY JUST BEGUN.

"THE MORNING SUN BREAKS THE HORIZON AND WARMS THE TEMPLE, AS IT HAS FOR CENTURIES."
"FOR NEARLY AS LONG, PEOPLE HAVE FLOCKED TO THE SHAOLIN MONASTERY TO HONE THEMSELVES SPIRITUALLY, MENTALLY, AND PHYSICALLY."
"LATELY, HOWEVER..."

"WELL, LET'S JUST SAY TIMES HAVE CERTAINLY CHANGED."
CAN I TAKE YOUR ORDER PLEASE?
CAN I TAKE YOUR ORDER PLEASE?
CAN I TAKE YOUR ORDER PLEASE?
"I HAVE BEEN CHIEF ASSISTANT TO MY SIFU, THE TEMPLE'S ABBOT, THE PAST FIVE YEARS. EACH MORNING, I WALK WITH HIM AS HE SURVEYS THE GROUNDS. THOUGH HE SAYS NOTHING, I KNOW HE IS TROUBLED."

STAY TUNED FOR THE CHALLENGE ROUND ON NEXT STAR OF SHAOLIN!
SALES HAVE BEEN STRONG THIS PAST MONTH, SIFU. LIKELY BECAUSE OF THE SHOW'S SEASON FINALE...
I SUPPOSE.

"THE COURTYARD, WHERE STUDENTS GATHER TO EXCHANGE IDEAS, PRACTICE TECHNIQUES, AND DISCUSS THE DHARMA."

"THE ARMORY, WHERE STUDENTS LABOR IN MASTERING THE MANY WEAPONS OF SHAOLIN."

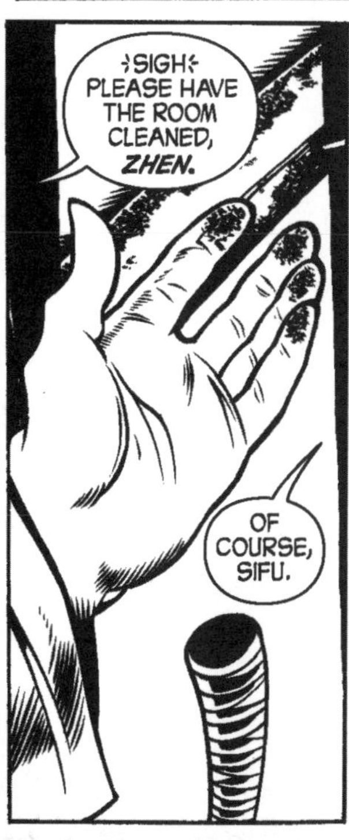
SIGH
PLEASE HAVE THE ROOM CLEANED, ZHEN.
OF COURSE, SIFU.

STORY: ROGER MA
PENCILS: DHEERAJ VERMA • INKS: TAK TOYOSHIMA

"THE INFIRMARY, WHERE BROKEN WARRIORS COME TO RECOVER. HOWEVER, MOST OF THOSE FILLING THE ROOM NOW... CANNOT BE HEALED."
HOW ARE YOU FEELING, ZHAO?
TIRED, BUT BETTER. THANK YOU, SIFU.

IS OUR GUESTS' CARE GOING WELL, BROTHER WANG?
IT'S GOING AS GOOD AS WE CAN MANAGE, SIFU.
THE DOCTOR FROM ZHENGZHOU HASN'T COME FOR HIS WEEKLY VISIT.
STRANGE, I WILL TRY TO CONTACT HIM TODAY.

MORE SHOW UP EVERY DAY SINCE YOU ANNOUNCED WE'D TAKE THEM IN. SIFU, OUR RESOURCES HERE ARE TAXED ENOUGH WITH OUR OWN INJURIES. WITH ALL DUE RESPECT, I DO NOT UNDERSTAND WHY WE MUST ALSO CARE FOR THE GANRANZHE.*
* PEOPLE INFECTED WITH HIV

THE BUDDHA TAUGHT US COMPASSION, BROTHER.
BESIDES, OUR COUNTRY ABANDONED THESE PEOPLE ONCE. WOULD YOU HAVE US DO SO AGAIN?

SIFU! PLEASE COME QUICKLY!

REPORTS ARE COMING IN FROM MAJOR CITIES ACROSS CHINA OF SIMULTANEOUS INCIDENTS OF CIVIL UNREST. LARGE ROAMING GANGS HAVE BEEN SEEN ATTACKING INNOCENT PEOPLE IN BRUTAL FASHION.
WITNESS REPORTS HAVE SAID THAT THE ATTACKERS SEEM TO BE SUFFERING FROM MASS HYSTERIA, AND ARE...EATING THE FLESH OF THEIR VICTIMS.
THIS VIDEO WAS UPLOADED ONLINE HOURS EARLIER, SHOWING AN ATTACK IN BEIJING.
THE GOVERNMENT IS MOBILIZING PLA FORCES TO ADDRESS THESE VIOLENT OUTBREAKS, SUSPECTED TO BE THE WORK OF...
...OF SEVERAL RADICAL DISSIDENT GROUPS. THEY ARE ENCOURAGING ALL CITIZENS TO REMAIN CALM. THE SITUATION... THE SITUATION IS UNDER CONTROL.
PLEASE CARRY ON WITH YOUR WORK.

"LATE IN THE EVENING, THE ABBOT CALLED THE SENIOR DISCIPLES TO HIS CHAMBERS."
WHAT CAN WE DO? WE KNOW NOTHING OF WHAT'S GOING ON BEYOND THESE TEMPLE WALLS. THE NEWS BROADCASTS SAY THINGS ARE UNDER CONTROL.
AND THEN THEY SUDDENLY WENT OFF THE AIR...AND YOU STILL BELIEVE THEM? IF WE WAIT TO SEE HOW THINGS TURN OUT, IT MAY BE TOO LATE.
WE NEED TO EVACUATE WHILE WE STILL CAN AND HEAD TOWARDS ZHENGZHOU!
YOU ASSUME THE CITY HAS NOT BEEN AFFLICTED, BROTHER CHOU. AND WHAT OF THOSE IN THE INFIRMARY? THERE ARE TOO MANY OF THEM TO MAKE OUR TRAVELS EASY.
THE GANRANZHE? WE CANNOT POSSIBLY CARE FOR THAT FILTH ON THE ROAD.
FOR ALL WE KNOW, THEY MAY BE THE CAUSE OF ALL THIS! THERE IS WORD THIS...MADNESS IS SPREAD THROUGH THE BLOOD!
SIFU, YOU HAVE BEEN SILENT.
PLEASE, WHAT WOULD YOU HAVE US DO?
REMEMBER, ALL OF YOU; OFTEN, THE OBSTACLE IS THE PATH. CLEAR THE ARMORY AND ASSEMBLE EVERYONE TOMORROW IN THE COURTYARD AT DAWN.
EVEN THOSE IN THE... INFIRMARY?
EVERYONE.
"THE COURTYARD AT DAWN..."
WHERE ARE THE REST OF US? WHERE'S BROTHER CHOU?
WE WERE TOLD TO ASSEMBLE EVERYONE.
THIS IS EVERYONE. APPARENTLY, MANY LEFT IN THE NIGHT, BACK HOME, BACK TO THE CITY, BACK TO ANYWHERE BUT HERE.
THOSE WHO DECIDED TO STAY, YOU HAVE MY GRATITUDE.
MANY OF YOU ARE EXPERTS WITH THESE WEAPONS—FOR SPORT AND EXHIBITION. BUT FOR OVER 300 YEARS, THE MONKS OF SHAOLIN HAVE NOT ENGAGED IN MORTAL COMBAT.
TIMES... HAVE CHANGED. AND WE MUST ONCE AGAIN CHANGE WITH THEM.

WE KNOW NOTHING OF THIS ENEMY WE FACE, EXCEPT THAT THEY CAN BE CUT. THEY CAN BLEED. THEY SEEM TO BE OUR FELLOW COUNTRYMEN— BUT WE MUST BE READY IF THEY ARE SOMETHING... ELSE.
SLICE!
PREPARE YOUR WEAPONS. BATTLE TRAINING BEGINS TODAY.
AND TO YOU, OUR GUESTS, AS YOU CAN SEE, OUR RANKS ARE THIN.
WE WOULD WELCOME YOUR HELP. I PLACE YOU IN THE CARE OF MY MOST TRUSTED MAN.
一 二 三

"WEEKS PASS, WITH NO FURTHER WORD FROM THE OUTSIDE WORLD. IT SEEMS AN INTERNET AND RADIO BLACKOUT IS IN FULL EFFECT. THIS IS NOT A CONCERN TO SIFU, AS HIS ONLY PRIORITY NOW IS TRAINING."
"BUT THE CONTINUED LACK OF NEWS LED OTHERS TO SLIP AWAY IN THE NIGHT--INCLUDING WANG, OUR LAST TRAINED HOSPITALLER. THOUGH I CAN'T HONESTLY SAY WE MISSED HIM."

"THE FIELD OF TRANQUILITY, 40 KILOMETERS FROM ZHENGZHOU."
BONG!
IT IS WHERE WE TRADITIONALLY HOLD EXHIBITIONS TO SHOW THE FORMIDABILITY OF SHAOLIN ARTS. TODAY, IT SEEMS, WE WILL BE TESTING THAT STRENGTH IN OTHER WAYS."

AAAOOOHMMM!
"THE SOUND OF THE BELLS ECHO ACROSS THE FIELD THROUGHOUT THE VALLEY AS WE CHANT FOR HOURS... AND WAIT."
AAAOOOHMMM!
WAAAAUUUUGGGGHH!

WAAAAUUUUUG GGGGHH!
"THE TIME HAS COME."

BE BRAVE, MY DISCIPLES!
SHAAAAAAA!
THUD!
SHING!
NGAAAAA!
DEMONS... THEY *CANNOT* BE KILLED!
KEEP FIGHTING! *DO NOT* GIVE UP!
FSSH!

SLAM!
THE BRAIN! ATTACK THE BRAIN!
SWISH!
GAAAHHHH!
eh?
THE GANRANZHE'S BLOOD... IT IS AS FATAL TO THE UNDEAD AS IT IS TO THE LIVING.

EVERYONE! OFF THE FIELD, NOW!
PROTECT THE CIVILIANS! WE MUST RETURN TO THE TEMPLE!
YOU FOUGHT BRAVELY TODAY, AND ANSWERED A QUESTION THAT MOST LIVE THEIR ENTIRE LIVES WITHOUT KNOWING. "AM I A COWARD?" YOU STARED DEATH IN THE FACE AND SURVIVED.
AND AS A RESULT OF THIS COURAGE, WE KNOW SOMETHING NEW: YOU OF THE GANRANZHE, WHOM OUR COUNTRYMEN HAVE DESPISED, MAY BE THE SALVATION OF OUR NATION, AND PERHAPS, OF HUMANITY.
I AM PROUD TO HAVE STOOD BY YOUR SIDE. REST WELL TONIGHT.
TOMORROW, WE HAVE MUCH TO SHARE WITH OUR COUNTRY.

OPEN UP!
IT'S WANG!
BAM BAM
WANG! YOU'VE RETURNED?
THANK THE HEAVENS THAT YOU'VE ARRIVED WITH ASSISTANCE! WE MUST SHARE WITH YOU WHAT WE'VE LEARNED—
IT'S AS I SAID, GENERAL: THEY'VE BEEN HARBORING DOZENS OF THE FILTHY DISEASED ONES WITHIN THE TEMPLE INFIRMARY.
NO, WANG, THE GANRANZHE ARE NOT THE CAUSE OF THE INFECTION... IN FACT—
BLAM!
SOLDIERS, CLEAR OUT THE TEMPLE.
END

OCCUPY ETHNIC FOODS

STORY & ART: TAK TOYOSHIMA

BUT IT IS *YOU* WHO ARE CONFUSED, SAUCY ONE. YOU SEE, WHILE MY FAMILY ROSE TO POWER IN JAPAN, OUR FATHER* WAS ACTUALLY....**TAIWANESE.**

*MOMOFUKU ANDO

THE RA-MEN AND RA-WOMEN OF OUR CLAN DO NOT "ASSIMILATE." WE **ABSORB** THE TASTES OF OTHERS, SO THAT WE MAY SEDUCE THEM.

NOW WE HAVE AMASSED A **FLASH-FRIED EMPIRE** THAT EXTENDS FAR BEYOND ORIENTAL FLAVORS. WE ARE A STAPLE FOOD OF THE 99%. WE DOMINATE COLLEGE STUDENT DIETS. **THE FUTURE IS OURS!**

WELL, I'M PROUD OF MY IDENTITY, NISSIN. I'VE STUCK WITH MY **CHINESE ROOTS**, AND I'LL STAND WITH MY ETHNIC BROTHERS!

THE SHADOW HERO

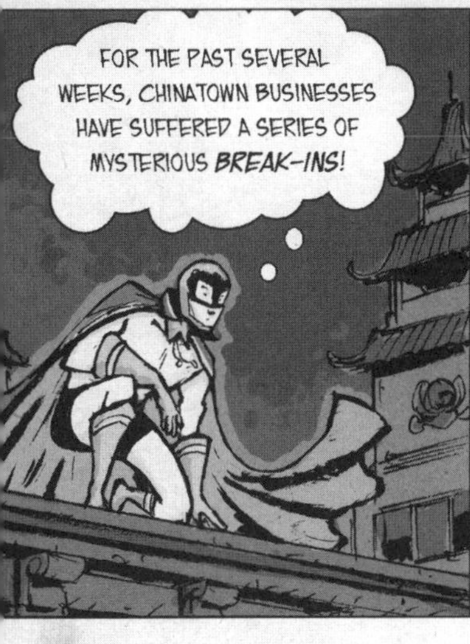
FOR THE PAST SEVERAL WEEKS, CHINATOWN BUSINESSES HAVE SUFFERED A SERIES OF MYSTERIOUS *BREAK-INS*!

NOW, AFTER PATROLLING THE STREETS FOR NIGHTS ON END...
KRSSH
...THE *GREEN TURTLE* WILL FINALLY HAVE SOME ANSWERS!

<HANK, WAIT!>*
<MA?!>
YANG LIEW

*Translated from Cantonese

THE SHADOW HERO

<MA, WHAT ARE YOU DOING HERE?!>
<I'VE ALWAYS WANTED TO WATCH YOU DO YOUR SUPERHERO WORK!>

<I GOT HOME EARLY TONIGHT AND THOUGHT TO MYSELF, WHY NOT RIGHT NOW?>
<WHAT IF SOMEONE SEES YOU?! YOU'LL COMPROMISE MY SECRET IDENTITY!>

<THAT'S WHY I BROUGHT A *MASK*!>
YANG LIEW

THE SHADOW HERO

<I ALSO BROUGHT YOU A *SNACK*! RED BEAN BUNS, YOUR FAVORITE!>

<GO HOME, MA. I NEED TO GO FIGHT CRIME.>
SIGH.
<FINE. I KNOW WHEN I'M NOT WANTED.>

<I'LL LEAVE THE BUNS UP HERE FOR YOU...>
<...IN CASE YOU GET *HUNGRY* AFTER YOU'RE DONE!>
YANG LIEW

STORY: GENE LUEN YANG
ART: SONNY LIEW

THE SHADOW HERO

THE SHADOW HERO

THE SHADOW HERO

FINALE
IT IS NOT LIKE HIM TO BE LATE.
IT IS NOT LIKE HIM TO BE PREDICTABLE.
BUT BROTHERS--THIS AFFORDS US OPPORTUNITY TO SPEAK, BEYOND THE REACH OF HIS DAMNABLE SHADOW. WHY DOES THE DARK ONE ROAM FREELY IN THE MORTAL REALM, WHILE WE WAIT UPON HIS MERCY?
HE OFFERED TO OPEN THE WAY FOR THE REST OF US TO FOLLOW. THERE IS RISK IN BEING DISCOVERED BY THESE MORTALS, AS OUR SISTER NGAU-YUN DISCOVERED. OUR DEAR, DEPARTED SISTER.
BE THAT AS IT MAY, BO-KWUN IS NOT ONE TO BE TRUSTED. WE MIGHT WISH TO FORMULATE... OTHER PLANS.
IT IS NOT LIKE HIM TO BE LATE.
GREETINGS, BROTHERS. FORGIVE THE DELAY. I BRING GOOD TIDINGS: SOON, YOU SHALL BE FREE TO WALK THE MORTAL PLANE.
WHY SHOULD WE BELIEVE YOU THIS TIME, DECEIVER?
"BECAUSE BROTHER, IN THE PAST..."
TROJANS vs SPARTANS
X-TRA LEAGUE FOOTBALL
"...THE UPSTART MORTALS WHO HAVE ABSORBED FRAGMENTS OF OUR POWER MANAGED TO THWART MY PLANS."
...DO WE EVEN KNOW THIS IS WHERE THEY HEADED? WE NEVER SHOULD'VE MADE THAT STOP IN PORTLAND, DICE.
HEY, WHEN NATURE CALLS, YOU GOTTA ANSWER.
LOOK, WE THINK THESE CREEPS WANNA KILL A BUNCH OF PEOPLE, RIGHT? WELL, THIS IS THE BIGGEST BUNCH OF PEOPLE ON THE PLANET RIGHT NOW.
COME ON! TODAY'S ULTRABOWL SUNDAY! DON'T EITHER OF YOU WATCH FOOTBALL?
SORRY, MORE OF A GOLF GUY.
UH... I PLAY IT ON THE YCUBE—DOES THAT COUNT?
I CAN'T BELIEVE I GOTTA SAVE THE WORLD WITH YOU TWO DORKS.

ILES ABOVE TROY CITY
MAYBE THIS WASN'T SUCH A GREAT IDEA.
G-GOTTA GET INSIDE.
CORRECTION. THIS DEFINITELY WASN'T SUCH A GREAT IDEA.
ABOVE TROYDOME
SIR, SECURITY FEED FROM THE CARGO PLANE.
INSIDE MISHIRA'S SHUTTLE
<YOUR HUMBLE SERVANT WISHES TO ALERT YOU THAT WE HAVE LANDED AT THE SELECTED SITE, DIVINE ONE.*>
<AND THE VRIL? HAS IT BEEN OBTAINED IN THE REQUISITE QUANTITIES?>
*TRANSLATED FROM THE JAPANESE
CHIKUSHO!
<THERE IS...A MINOR DISTRACTION.>
<IT WILL BE RESOLVED IMMEDIATELY.>

INFORM THE SHADOWTHIEF THAT IF THE SHIPMENT IS NOT SECURED, I WILL USE THOSE BLADES OF HERS TO CARVE MY SEPUKKU NOTE ON HER BACK. FROM THE INSIDE.
THIS WAS THE WORST IDEA IN THE HISTORY OF BAD IDEAS!!
UH, SIR, YESSIR, SIR.
OKAY, SIS...I TRACKED THE PSYCHIC FINGERPRINT YOU SENSED IN YOUR STUPID PIECE OF GLASS...
STUPID?!
...YEAH, GUES WHAT, THES GUYS ARE BA NEWS...NOV TELL MOM TO PORT ME O OF HERE!
WHY?!?
...BECAUSE A CREE OLD DUDE JUST DUSTED SOMEON IN FRONT OF ME, AND I GET THE SENS SOMETHING NAST IS RIGHT BEHIND THIS DOORWAY!
DID YOU TRULY THINK I WAS NOT AWARE OF YOUR PRESENCE, MORTAL MORSEL? I WOULD CONSUME YOU SLOWLY, BUT YOU HAVE SKILLS THAT COULD BE OF USE--IF PROPERLY...TWISTED.
GAHHHH! TENTACLES!
HELLO? HELLO?? VERNON!
SLLIGGEE
BACK ON THE CARGO PLANE
YEESH. HOPE WE DIDN'T NEED THAT.
SNATCH
SORRY, NINJA LADY: SWORD VERSUS CUTTING-EDGE NANOTECH? SWORD LOSE.
SHATTER

KRRREEES
AWAY, INSECTS. THE DARK ONE MUST NOT BE ALLOWED TO RECEIVE THIS SHIPMENT.
WHAT THE--?
SHHHHKKKK
HEY...
...NOT SO FAST!
SCRIIITCH
SCRIIITCH
I'M TOUGHER'N I LOOK.
SORRY, HOODIE, GOT SOME UNFINISHED BUSINESS WITH THIS MOOK.
OK, RAVI, IT'S BASHIN' TIME... ROUND TWO!
...WHO ARE YOU GUYS?
THE NAME'S
HHHHIIIIIIOOOOEEE...!
THWAKKKKK
I CARRY TWO SWORDS, PREY... AND I ONLY DRAW THE SHADOW BLADE WHEN IT IS TIME TO KILL. ITS EDGE IS A SINGLE ATOM WIDE. I MIGHT MAKE A JOKE ABOUT "CUTTING-EDGE NANOTECH"--IF I HAD A SENSE OF HUMOR.
NOOOOOOO!
MISHIRA-DONO: I HAVE THE BURIRU, BUT I REQUIRE SOME ASSISTANCE FROM BROTHER SQUID.
...DIDN'T WE DROP BUILDING ON YOU, HIDEOUS ONE?
SHHHHHAAKTTTT

EJECT... CREATE EXOSKELETON!
BURIRU AND SHADOWTHIEF SECURED, MISHIRA-DONO.
OUCH.
CATCH, LITTLE MAN.
UH, THANKS.
CAN NICE KITTY PUT "LITTLE MAN" ON GROUND NOW?
KHOOM!
WOW!
KRSSHH
SMASH!
YEAH, DOUBLE WOW!
...I THINK I WILL NEED REINFORCEMENTS, MISHIRA-DONO.
DELAY THEM, SHADOWTHIEF. I MUST ESCORT THE EMPEROR TO HIS APPOINTMENT WITH DESTINY.
<DONE!>

VIE--TAKE MOM AND GO AFTER THE CAR.
DICE--TAKE KAT AND GO AFTER THE CAR.
I CAN HANDLE THESE GUYS.
RYAN SUDA. I'VE GOT THE BIG DUDE.
VALERIE CHANG. I'LL GET THE LITTLE DUDES. BUT EASE UP ON THE BIG DUDE–PRETTY SURE THAT'S MY BROTHER.
DEFINITELY DON'T SEE THE FAMILY RESEMBLANCE.
TALK MORE LATER?
OKAY, NEIGHBOR, YOUR SISTER WANTS ME TO HOLD BACK A LITTLE, SO LET'S START WITH THIIIS...FORE!
CRUNCH!!!
HUH. BETTER MOVE UP TO A TWO-IRON.
OKAY, WAND, I NEED EVERYTHING YOU'VE GOT. NO CHANTS. NO POSES. NO FAIRY GLITTER. NOTHING THAT'S GONNA EMBARRASS ME IN FRONT OF THE HOT GUY OVER THERE THROWING CARS AROUND.
WHAT YOU'RE ASKING FOR IS IMPOSSIBLE, MISTRESS. IT'S COMPLETELY AGAINST MAGICAL GIRL PROTOCOL--
DO IT AND I PROMISE TO WEAR THAT RIDONKULOUS PINK OUTFIT YOU'VE BEEN NAGGING ME ABOUT.
...DONE.

NOW THIS I COULD GET INTO.
I'M A MELEE WEAPON! I FEEL SO BUTCH.
SHUT UP AND CHOP-CHOP NINJA, WAND.
DO NOT THINK YOU CAN ESCAPE, DARK ONE--
<BEGONE>.
AGGH!! HM. AS THE MORTALS SAY... IT IS TIME FOR -- PLAN B.
LOOK ALIVE, YOU'RE TOO CLOSE...
DeMONNA
DAMMIT, DICE! TOLD YOU WE WERE FOLLOWING TOO CLOSE!
NOT MY FAULT: THAT SITH LORD GUY GESTURED AT ME AND ALL OF A SUDDEN I LOST CONTROL--AND, UH, ON THE SUBJECT OF "THINGS I CAN'T CONTROL," I JUST WANNA APOLOGIZE IN ADVANCE, KAT...
OH, MY GOD, DICE! WITH ALL THIS STUFF GOING ON?
LOOK, I'M A GUY, OK?
DIE.
BLAM.

MY SUBJECTS: THIS SUBSTANCE, VRIL, INFUSED IN TINY AMOUNTS THROUGHOUT YOUR BLOOD AND BONE, IS WHAT GIVES YOU YOUR POWERS.
GOLDFIELD MINE V.R.I.L. SAMPLES
BUT YOUR POWERS WERE ORIGINALLY OUR POWER— MINE AND MY SIBLINGS" RELEASED IN SHATTERING THE SEAL THAT BARRED US FROM THIS DIMENSION.
AND SO, WITH THIS GRAND LENS, I AM ABLE TO PLACE YOU UNDER ABSOLUTE CONTROL. WITH YOU AS MY PUPPET ARMY, NONE DARE STAND AGAINST ME.
ON THE CONTRARY, BROTHER: THREE DARE.
WE NOW KNOW THAT IT WAS NEVER YOUR PLAN TO RELEASE US FROM BONDAGE— YOU SEEK TO WIN THIS WORLD FOR YOURSELF!
ZZZZZZT!
ZZZZZZT!
WUMP!
SLAMM!
SLAM
BUT AS YOU NOTED, THE VRIL'S POWER IS NOT YOURS ALONE. AND THOUGH WE ARE FORCED TO WORK THROUGH THESE CRIPPLED MORTAL SHELLS, TOGETHER, WE ARE YOUR EQUAL, BO-KWUN.
CRAP. HOW DO WE EVEN KNOW WHAT SIDE WE'RE ON?
WE ARE ON THE SIDE OF LIFE. THEY ARE ON THE SIDE OF DEATH.

HEY, RYAN. BEEN A WHILE, HUH? THIS HERE'S JIMSON. HE DUG ME OUTTA THAT CRATER I MADE BACK THERE.
SERIOUSLY, I PLOW INTO THE GROUND FROM FIVE THOUSAND FEET AND YA GUYS JUST DITCH ME? UNBELIEVABLE. WHO DOES THAT?
YOU LANDED HEAD FIRST. WE FIGURED YOU'D BE FINE.
WE DO NOT HAVE TIME TO BANTER, FRIENDS. THE EVILS WITHIN MUST NOT BE ALLOWED TO TRIUMPH.
SORRY, GUYS...I GOT NOTHING. MY GEAR'S FLATLINED, AND I'M PRETTY MUCH DEPENDENT ON CUTTING-EDGE NANOTECH...
...OKAY, YEAH, I'M GOOD.
YOU DARE LAY HANDS ON ZHI-LIK, MORTAL WHELP?
HANDS, NO. SWORD, YES.
SLISH!
UGH!
TUD!
INFINITE PURITY STRIKE!... WAND, TELL THE TRUTH: YOU MAKE UP THESE INCANTATION NAMES JUST TO EMBARRASS ME, RIGHT?
IT IS MY ONE JOY IN LIFE, MISTRESS.
AGHH!
LISTEN WELL, YOUNG ONE. WITH THE FALL OF THE THREE, ALL THOSE AROUND US WILL COME UNDER THE CONTROL OF THE MANIPULATOR--EXCEPT US. MY POWERS ARE ELEMENTAL IN NATURE, WHILE OURS ARE LOCKED IN THE DEVICES YOU WEAR; OUR VEINS DO NOT FLOW WITH VRIL.
SO WHEN I GIVE THE SIGNAL...

DeMON
GO!!!
zzZZZTCHHHH!!!
THE LENS!
MADAM, NOW! OPEN A PORTAL ABOVE THE PLATFORM!
TO--TO WHERE?
TO NOWHERE!
WHA-- WHAT ARE YOU--
NGGHH!

AND NOW, YOUNG ONE, I MUST BEG YOUR ASSISTANCE. WITHIN YOU FLOWS ELEMENTAL FIRE. ONLY YOU HAVE THE POWER TO DO WHAT MUST BE DONE.
DESTROY ME.
NO WAY, MAN. I CAN'T KILL YOU--
I WILL NOT DIE-- MERELY ABANDON MY CURRENT PHYSICAL SHAPE. ONLY A LIVING BARRIER CAN KEEP THE MANIPULATOR AND HIS KIND FROM RETURNING TO THIS WORLD. CENTURIES AGO, THE AIR ELEMENTAL SATALAN AND HIS HUMAN ALLY, ZHANG SANFENG, GAVE THEMSELVES TO FORM THE FIRST GREAT SEAL-- THE MIRROR OF DIVINE IMMORTALS.
NOW A NEW PAIR OF MORTAL SOULS, ONE ELEMENTAL, ONE HUMAN, MUST REPLACE IT.
YOU MEAN... YOU AND ME?
NO, CHILD. THERE IS ALREADY A HUMAN SOUL PLEDGED TO THIS DEED.
NOW HURRY. YOUR FRIENDS WILL NOT BE ABLE TO CONTAIN THE MANIPULATOR'S TRUE FORM MUCH LONGER.
JH
THERE HAD TO BE ANOTHER WAY. HE DIDN'T HAFTA BE ALONE.
DAVID...I DON'T THINK HE WAS ALONE.
IT HAS BEEN TOO LONG, MY FRIEND.
GOT PLENTY OF TIME TO CATCH UP, JIMSON.
GOT ALL THE TIME IN THE WORLD.
JH

BLANK CANVAS.

N EMPTY ROOM.

TO SOME, THESE SPEAK OF DESPAIR AND ISOLATION. TO OTHERS...
...THEY REPRESENT OPPORTUNITY.

N VILCEK.

"I WAS BORN IN 1933 IN BRATISLAVA, IN WHAT WAS THEN CZECHOSLOVAKIA--"
Bratislava
COUNTRY THAT NO LONGER EXISTS."

"I WAS A BOY WHEN THE NAZIS BEGAN TO SPREAD ACROSS EUROPE. THOUGH THEY WERE NOT RELIGIOUS, AS JEWS, MY PARENTS FEARED BEING SENT TO THE CAMPS AT ANY TIME. AS A PRECAUTION, THEY PLACED ME IN AN ORPHANAGE RUN BY CATHOLIC NUNS."
"LATER, WHEN MY FATHER JOINED THE RESISTANCE, MY MOTHER AND I FLED TO THE COUNTRY, WHERE WE WERE CARED FOR BY A SYMPATHETIC SLOVAK FAMILY. THESE WERE THE FIRST TIMES I WAS BLESSED BY THE KINDNESS OF STRANGERS--BUT FAR FROM THE LAST."

RICA VILCEK.
AND I WERE
N IN THE SAME
BUT WE DID
MEET UNTIL
R COLLEGE.
HAT TIME,
NAZIS
E GONE,
A NEW
DOW HAD
EN ACROSS
NATION."

"UNDER THE COMMUNISTS, SOCIETY BECAME A PLACE OF SECRETS AND WHISPERS."
"I STUDIED ART HISTORY IN COLLEGE, AND MANAGED TO AVOID GETTING DENOUNCED. BUT NOW AND AGAIN, MY CLASSMATES WOULD DISAPPEAR, WITHOUT EXPLANATION."
"IN THOSE DAYS, AN ANONYMOUS LETTER FROM A STRANGER COULD MEAN EJECTION FROM SCHOOL...OR WORSE."

HAD BEEN INTRODUCED BY A FRIEND,
LOST CONTACT WHEN JAN LEFT FOR
UDY EXCHANGE IN MOSCOW. WE
ONNECTED BY CHANCE, WHEN JAN
ED THE MUSEUM WHERE I
KED. WITHIN A YEAR, HE'D
POSED--AND I ACCEPTED."
"FACING A DIM AND UNCERTAIN FUTURE, WE AGREED WE WANTED TO FIND A WAY TO LEAVE."
"A FEW YEARS AFTER WE MARRIED, I GOT AN INVITATION TO VISIT VIENNA--JUST 40 MILES FROM BRATISLAVA, BUT IN THOSE DAYS, IT MIGHT AS WELL HAVE BEEN THE MOON."
238900 miles
Vienna
40 MILES
Bratislava
Austria
"THE GOVERNMENT USUALLY WOULD NOT LET FAMILY GO ABROAD TOGETHER. WE WERE SHOCKED WHEN WE RECEIVED PERMISSION TO GO."

STORY: JEFF YANG
ART: WENDY XU

"BUT WE HAD TO LEAVE EVERYTHING BEHIND."
YES, YES...
YOU ARE ATTENDING THE OPERA IN VIENNA? I MYSELF AM AN OPERA FAN!
"WE COULDN'T EVEN TELL OUR HOSTS, FEARING THEY'D WITHDRAW THE INVITATION!"
...Der Höller Rache...
"AND OF COURSE, WE COULD NOT STAY LONG. BUT WHAT COUNTRY WOULD TAKE US, WITH NO PASSPORT OR MONEY?"
"THE ANSWER WAS...AMERICA."
"ON ARRIVING IN THE U.S., I ACCEPTED AN OFFER FROM NEW YORK UNIVERSITY."
IT'S WONDERFUL, THEY'VE HEARD OF MY WORK!
A JOB, ALREADY?
"I KNEW NOTHING ABOUT HOW RESEARCH WAS CONDUCTED HERE IN THE U.S. I WAS SURPRISED WHEN THEY TOLD ME IF I WANTED TO DO MY WORK, I WOULD HAVE TO FIND MONEY ON MY OWN."
WE CAN GIVE YOU THIS LAB. EVERYTHING ELSE, YOU HAVE TO FUND WITH GRANTS.
"IT WAS A CHALLENGE. BUT ALSO...AN OPPORTUNITY."
"I TOO FOUND A JOB--AS A CLERK TYPIST AT THE METROPOLITAN MUSEUM OF ART."
YOU'RE OVERQUALIFIED, BUT IT'S ALL WE HAVE RIGHT NOW.
"IT WASN'T MUCH...BUT IT WAS AN OPPORTUNITY. WITHIN A YEAR, I HAD BEEN PROMOTED TO THE CURATORIAL TEAM."
"IN 1989, 25 YEARS AFTER COMING TO THIS COUNTRY, M LAB HAD A BREAK THROUGH, HELPING TO CREATE A DRUG THAT'S NOW ONE OF THE MOST POWERFUL TOOLS WE HAVE TO FIGHT CHRONIC AUTOIMMUNE DISEASE."
"THE DRUG PROVED VERY SUCCESSFUL."
WE'VE DONE WELL. WE NEED TO GIVE BACK.
"WE DECIDED TO USE THE MONEY TO SUPPORT AND CELEBRATE OTHERS LIKE US--WHO CAME HERE FROM DISTANT LANDS, SEEKING FREEDOM, HOPE...AND A NEW PLACE TO CALL HOME."
"IN 2000, WE LAUNCHED THE VILCEK FOUNDATION, FUNDING CULTURAL PROGRAMS LIKE THIS BOOK..."
"...AND GIVING ANNUAL PRIZES TO IMMIGRANTS WHO'VE MADE GREAT STRIDES FOR THIS COUNTRY..."
"BECAUSE IF YOU LOOK AROUND, YOU'LL SEE THAT NEWCOMERS ARE MAKING SOME OF OUR MOST IMPORTANT ADVANCES--IN SCIENCE, THE ARTS..."
"...AND IN THE COMICS!"
WHERE WOULD COMICS BE WITHO IMMIGRANTS
USING CARTOONS TO TELL IMMIGRANT STORIES. WHAT WILL THEY THINK OF NEXT?
STAN JIM L
ARE THEY BROTHERS?
THEY'RE BROTHE
THE SECRET IDENTITIES UNIVERSE WOULD LIKE TO EXPRESS ITS THANKS TO THE VILCEK FOUNDATION FOR ITS GENEROUS SUPPORT OF SHATTERED...
YOU GAVE US THE POWER TO FLY!